G000123389

On His Heart

Our High Priest's Loving Care

On His Heart

Our High Priest's Loving Care

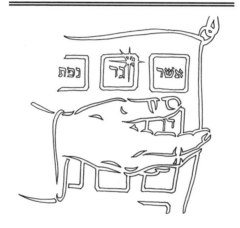

MADGE BECKON

GOSPEL FOLIO PRESS
P. O. Box 2041, Grand Rapids MI 49501-2041

Published by GOSPEL FOLIO PRESS
P. O. Box 2041, Grand Rapids, MI 49501-2041

ISBN 1-882701-59-3

Cover design by J. B. Nicholson, Jr.

PRINTED IN THE UNITED STATES OF AMERICA

ACKNOWLEDGMENTS

Thanks to my daughter, Esther, for the many hours she has given to help me with the writing of this book. Her contributions have been welcome and most helpful. Being together so many hours at the computer has been a mutual blessing to us as we made corrections and she sought to clarify what I really wanted to say.

I greatly appreciate the wonderful cooperation from the staff of Gospel Folio Press who made *On His Heart* a reality.

DEDICATION

To my granddaughter, Heather, and her "jewel" of a husband, Stephan Hunt. Heather, my one and only granddaughter, has been the joy of ten to me and Steve has added much since he joined the family. It is my prayer that they will take up the mantles dropped by their grandfathers who served the Lord as missionaries, Steve's in South America and Heather's in China and Japan. May they, too, follow the Lord wholly and seek to serve Him wherever the Lord may place them.

INTRODUCTION

My purpose in writing *On His Heart* is to echo the adoring exclamation of Mary Magdalene when she saw our resurrected Lord before the open tomb: *"Jesus saith unto her, Mary. She turned herself, and saith unto Him, Rabboni; which is to say Master."*

My Master has been much more than a Master. As the Father, He has provided (Mt. 7:11). Like a mother, He has comforted me by singing me to sleep many nights (Zeph. 3:17; Isa. 66:12, 13). As a husband, He has been faithful and kind beyond description (Isa. 54:5). Like a son, He has charged many to look after my needs (Jn. 19:27). As my Physician, He has prescribed the balm of Gilead countless times, expressing His personal interest and concern (Jer. 8:22). And as Teacher He has been oh so patient (Ps. 143:10)!

I can't begin to express all that is on my heart, so permit me to borrow the words of David in Psalm 138:

> *I will praise Thee with my whole heart...I will worship toward Thy holy temple, and praise Thy Name for Thy lovingkindness and for Thy truth; for Thou hast magnified Thy Word above all Thy Name. In the day when I cried Thou answeredst me, and strengthenedst me with strength in my soul...Though the Lord be high, yet hath He respect unto the lowly...Though I walk in the midst of trouble, Thou wilt revive me...The Lord will perfect that which concerneth me. Thy mercy, O Lord, endureth for ever.*

What a delight it is to serve my Master. My heart echoes the words of the slave expressed in Exodus 21:5-6: *"I love my mas-*

ter, I will not go out free...and his master shall bore his ear through with an awl and he shall serve Him for ever."

I am looking forward to remaining in the Master's house where I can serve Him forever. I'm sure you also eagerly await the promise of Revelation 22:3-4: *"And there shall be no more curse...And His servants shall serve Him: and they shall see His face; and His name shall be in their foreheads."*

It's all because of Calvary,

MADGE BECKON
Englewood, CO
1999

CONTENTS

1
ON HIS HEART

Wouldn't it be frightening to be forced to put our eternal future into the hands of an all-powerful God whom we could not trust? It is unthinkable to imagine ourselves in the hands of an evil authority. The closer I get to that eternal day, the more thankful I am that "the God whose I am and whom I serve" has proven Himself trustworthy! It is also wonderful to know that God has a heart—that He has feelings toward us as a loving Father. He keeps us constantly on His heart and in His hands. Isaiah 49:13-16 states this clearly. In fact, God gives us His Word:

Sing, O heavens, and be joyful, O earth, and break forth into singing, O mountains; for the Lord hath comforted His people, and will have mercy upon His afflicted. But Zion said, the Lord hath forsaken me, and the Lord hath forgotten me. Can a woman forget her nursing child, that she should not have compassion on the son of her womb? Yea, they may forget, yet will I not forget thee. Behold, I have engraved thee upon the palms of My hands; thy walls are continually before Me.

It is one thing to read the above portion of Scripture and assent to it with our minds, but it is another thing to believe it in our hearts. And it is even harder to wait on God while He orchestrates this truth in our lives! My life would have been much more stable earlier in my Christian experience if my foresight had been as good as my hindsight, if I had been able to wait on God's loving heart.

This morning I recalled my feelings when as a seven-year-old child I was sitting in the front seat between my father and his friend from whom he had asked advice. Dad was facing a terribly important business decision. That night he had to decide whether to tell the drillers to stop drilling or not. Money had run out and they had not hit oil. He had to give the final word.

I sat in the car as the two of them went to discuss the issue with the drillers. It was dark outside, but the atmosphere in the car was much darker when they came back with the news that Dad had decided to stop drilling. I knew my daddy was hurting because he was very quiet for the rest of the evening.

As a young child, I couldn't begin to understand the serious implications this decision would have for our family.

Later, I learned that Dad had invested the entire profit from the coal business he had sold just weeks before into that oil well. His plan was to use the oil well proceeds to prepare for the ministry. That night he knew his plans to support our family while he attended seminary had just gone down the drain. Dad had been saved only a little over a year at that time and mother had been saved only a matter of months. I can imagine the questions that must have flooded their minds. Why would the Lord permit such a thing when my father had good motives? What was his next step to be?

From all outward appearances, the Lord had not had compassion on my father, nor had He rewarded him for his good intentions. In fact, things went from bad to worse. That night was merely the beginning of a long time of testing for him and our family. As a result of scarlet fever, my brother developed a serious heart condition. On top of this blow, my grandparents disowned my mother when she left their family religion and was baptized. (Later their relationship was fully restored.) Then the depression hit! This, too, must have been a terrific blow to my parents, but it didn't stop their desire to follow Christ. Dad was determined to answer the call to become a pastor and to serve the Lord in that way. He would not allow himself to be distracted.

In order to feed our family during those difficult years, my dad took a job as an insurance agent. For the first few years he commuted from the city to a neighboring town. He substituted going to seminary by taking correspondence courses from a well-known Bible college. Some of my earliest memories are of Dad poring over his books at the first crack of dawn before he left for work. I used to peek in on him, and I remember his ready smile and wave as I passed by the door.

One of his first clients in his new business was a lady who operated a bean factory in her garage. She picked out the bad beans with an electric vacuum as they rolled by on the belt operated by a foot treadle. After he sold her the insurance policy, he started witnessing to her. He found a receptive heart, so every week when he went to pick up her premium, he told her a little more about the Lord and salvation. To shorten the story, she became a Christian and immediately began earnestly witnessing to her family. Two of her three daughters also accepted Christ as their Saviour. Then others in town took notice of the change in this family and opened their ears to the gospel. As a result, they started a Bible class in her home.

In less than a year, it was evident that the Bible class had grown so much that a place to meet larger than the woman's living room was needed. At about the same time, news of an elderly couple—who were seen every Wednesday night on the steps of an old dilapidated church building—reached the class. Dad arranged to stay over one Wednesday evening to confirm the story.

As reported, he found the couple having an old-fashioned prayer meeting right on the steps of the church building. He joined them, and their hearts bonded in their desire to see the doors opened once again. When he drove them home, he learned that they walked two miles and back every week, when the weather permitted. They had been praying that God would send someone He could use to open the old building and rebuild the congregation.

13

It didn't take long to inquire about details. Permission was soon granted to relocate the Bible class in the church building. Paint was too great a luxury in those days, so the cobwebs were brushed down and the walls were whitewashed. Former members were contacted, willing hands were offered, and the work was completed. The next Sunday morning, regular services resumed. It mattered little that Dad had no credentials, nor that the pianist could only play two songs that first morning. There was great rejoicing! The weekly Bible class continued there every Wednesday night as well.

Last summer, sixty-five years after the events described above, I was thrilled to tears by a surprise visit from a missionary family I'd never met. Two days before a friend's wedding I received a desperate phone call asking if I could possibly find space to sleep a missionary family of five. The family was from the field in which my friend (the bride) had served as a school teacher. They were home on furlough and wanted very much to attend her wedding.

The evening they arrived, the wife was in the kitchen helping me with dinner. To make conversation, she asked me from what part of the country I had come. Her eyes lit up when I told her I was born in Grand Rapids, Michigan. I went on to explain that my family moved to a small town about twenty miles east of there. When she asked which town it was, her eyes grew even bigger, and my response prompted a third question. Which church had I attended as a child? When I told her, her eyes popped out of her head. She said, "I grew up there, and that is our supporting church! We're on our way there now!" Her husband was scheduled to give a missionary report there the following week.

I was so thrilled, I burst into tears. When I could control myself enough to talk, I explained that their supporting church was the group of believers the Lord had established through my father's ministry more than sixty-five years before. I saw this family as part of the fruit from Dad's service for the Lord. Now they, in turn, are bearing fruit on the mission field. She also informed me that the congregation has built a beautiful, new building.

Later, after my guests had gone and I was alone, I thought about how God had orchestrated all the adverse circumstances my family experienced to make this possible. All of a sudden I could see how greatly God had worked. I remembered my Dad's testimony in which he had said that the liquid, black gold that never came out of the hole in the ground would be replaced with God's pure gold. I saw Dad and Mom as rich people indeed. They had literally taken John's advice in Revelation 3:18, *"I counsel thee to buy of Me gold tried in the fire, that thou mayest be rich."*

My Dad ended his testimony by saying, "I would not exchange God's gold for all the liquid black gold that was ever pumped out of the earth." Today he wouldn't have to say that only by faith. Now he could see some of the gold by sight.

God indeed had my parents on His heart the whole time. Their experiences were good training for me. God also had all of our names engraved upon the palms of His hands (Isa. 49:16), including the names of the dear elderly couple who had prayed so faithfully for those church doors to be opened again.

2
FIRST IMPRESSIONS

As my daughter Eunice and I took off from Denver International Airport we looked at each other and said, "Pinch me." We could hardly believe we were actually on our way to Japan where we would join a tour group bound for Israel. An assembly of believers in Takasaki had invited us to travel with a group from Japan, more than three-fourths of whom were from that assembly. This was my third visit to Japan since I retired in 1987 and my first trip to Israel. Eunice had left Japan as a high school graduate thirty years before and had only been back once, eighteen years previous.

I had felt right from the moment I received the invitation that it would be a special time for us, and I was not disappointed. I knew I had the right traveling partner, for Eunice looked after me to the point of embarrassment. When I ran out of steam, she took over the conversation for me. As a missionary wife and mother, I had often suffered from a divided heart. Trying to sort out the responsibility to my family from the work of the Lord was sometimes very difficult. This visit proved to me that the Lord never intended competition between the two. He had them equally on His heart, but He did have His priorities as to timing. Now I see that He is giving me the very best of two wholes rather than two halves—the blessings of family and the blessings of Japanese believers. The trip back to Japan was a combination of the two.

My first impression upon meeting the Christians who met us at Narita Airport was their joy in the Lord and the love they showed to us. It was great to be with them again. The grati-

17

tude for our having come to Japan, expressed by so many Christians, defies description. On the three-and-one-half-hour ride to Takasaki, we caught up on the latest news of individuals we knew. As I always do, I felt compelled to rally more prayer support for the believers on my return to the United States. The struggles and daily battles they face are every bit as severe today as they were when we first set foot on Japanese soil fifty years ago.

After two days of resting and adjusting to jet lag, we went to our first scheduled ladies' meeting. They had allotted ten minutes for Eunice to give her greetings before I spoke because they didn't know how her Japanese had fared during her long time away from Japan. As she began to share about the Lord's dealings with her, her facility in Japanese began to come back to everyone's surprise. Later, two or three of the women came up to me to say what a blessing the sharing of her experiences was to them. They tearfully explained that she had encouraged them to patiently wait for God to work in the lives of their children. Many of the women face dealing with rebellious teens. Eunice had mentioned she had not left Japan because she didn't love Japan. She *did* love Japan. It was home to her, but she left because she was not inclined to follow the Lord at the time. They knew this was true.

The struggle to follow the Lord is one with which many Japanese believers are familiar. Among the group meeting us at the airport, for example, was a middle-aged believer who was the "first-fruits" of the Sunday school work. I had not seen her in years. She was saved, baptized, and had perfect attendance until she entered her teens. I remember the day she told me with tears that her father forbade her to attend any longer because it would hinder her chances for a good marriage. I pled with her to put God first. She said she must obey her father if she wanted to finish her education. She made her choice. She married an unsaved man and now has two teenage daughters. She finally came to the decision that no matter what the cost, she must follow Christ. The Lord has worked so greatly in her heart as she has in Eunice's.

Another impression came from a visit with a middle-aged bachelor who had spent many hours in our home. He had a personal history of struggling to keep his spiritual nose above water. As a result, he was always in some degree of despondency. We knew he was seeking God, but he never could quite stand by faith upon His promises. Although he believed God was who He claimed to be, living by his beliefs was too great a sacrifice to make.

The night his mother died was the turning point in his life. The family had gathered to make the funeral arrangements and discuss plans for their future. Everyone decided that he should lead the procession and be the first to place the offering of incense to the spirit of his mother at the Buddhist funeral. After all, he was the oldest son and this was his responsibility if he was to inherit the family home. He tried to explain his position as a believer in the Lord Jesus Christ, but words would not come out because he knew his life before them had not been a positive example of what a true believer should be. At the same time, he did not feel that he could deny Christ in order to comply with his family's wishes.

Only God knew the depth of the struggle he experienced. His whole future was at stake. Either he would do as his family requested and accept full responsibility for his father, participating in the rites associated with it, or he would have to leave home and start life over again.

He was absolutely speechless, shook his head and burst into tears. He didn't have the strength of the Lord to declare openly his refusal. Twice he was to the point of agreeing with them, but the words only got to his throat and would not come out. He left the room and the family counsel broke up. Each member left in great anger.

After a miserable sleepless night, he was still convinced he could not comply with his family's wishes. He was in a quandary about how to refuse without hurting his father whom he loved dearly. He didn't want to deny Christ either. However, the Lord graciously undertook for him. While he was still praying about the matter and trying to find a suitable solution, his father came into his room early the next morning with the news that he would excuse him from the Buddhist rituals if he took over the responsibility of cooking and cleaning for him after working hours. He could continue to stay with him and they would work out the details at a later date. He was also excused from leading the funeral procession.

As he told me this story with great gestures, the sparkle in his eyes proved that his decision had been one pleasing to God even though it was made in great human weakness and timidity. Through this tremendous exercise of soul-searching, he realized how close he had come to denying Christ for a house and family! He saw that he was truly a sinner and for the first time in his experience he was convicted in his heart. I stared at this dear brother in disbelief, because I had been sure of his salvation years ago. He explained to me how he had always thought of his sins as merely failures and mistakes but now clearly knew he needed God's forgiveness. He finally saw compromise as real sin and now appreciates the cross of Christ in a new way. He identified with Peter in his denial of Christ because he had been as close to it as Peter was.

There was deep feeling in this man's voice as he introduced his father to me at a dinner party our very first Sunday night back in Japan. The father is still not saved, but he seems to have lost much of his resistance to the gospel. Our brother told me, with the biggest smile I have ever seen on his face, that he was beginning to feel the need to bring a bride into the home to help him out. Will you add him and all the Japanese believers to your prayer list? Their spiritual struggles will only be won through spiritual warfare (see 2 Cor. 10:4).

On Christmas morning, we left Japan for Israel. After a stopover in Switzerland for the night, we arrived in Tel Aviv.

My first impression of Israel on the bus ride to our hotel in Caesarea was the beauty of the land. From the many pictures I had seen, I always imagined Israel to be barren desert. But we were seeing miles and miles of lush green date palms, banana plantations, orange and grapefruit groves, and olive trees resulting from good irrigation and deep wells. As I saw with my own eyes the gorgeous roses of every color it brought to mind the passage in Isaiah 35:1, *"The wilderness and the solitary place shall…blossom as the rose."*

It confirmed the truth that God's Word stands—not that we need to see the land before we believe it. On several occasions I felt very strong emotions as God brought special passages of Scripture to mind. What He had prophesied had been fulfilled and it gave me renewed confidence that what has not yet been fulfilled will also come to pass.

The first tremendous feelings came from seeing the remains of Chorazin as it stands today. I was extremely conscious of Christ's words: *"Woe unto thee, Chorazin!"* The city was cursed and remains in that state, along with the other two cursed cities, Capernaum and Bethsaida (Lk. 10:13-16) even today. Jesus has the power to bring to pass just what He says He will.

While visiting Qumran where the Dead Sea scrolls were found, and later in the museum in Jerusalem, I was also deeply impressed. Christ had said in Matthew 5:18: *"For verily I say unto you, Till heaven and earth pass, one jot or one tittle shall in no way pass from the law, till all be fulfilled."*

The love the Jewish people have for the ancient scrolls of God's Word is astonishing. They have spent great amounts of money to ensure its preservation. It was a thrill to me to think that God preserved the scrolls in spite of the ravages of time and the elements of nature until man had the technology to preserve them through moisture and temperature control.

Deuteronomy 6:4-13—a passage dealing with the influence God and His Word should have on our families—came to mind as Eunice and I stood side by side at what is reputed to be David's tomb. I remembered the day my husband Gifford and I had read that passage together and claimed those words for our family, too. Feeling the very presence of God at the moment, and believing in His power to work in lives today, brought tears that were hard to control. I was in the company of many other people who unashamedly showed their emotions too. All around me, Jews were crying with great feelings, begging God to send His Messiah with peace to restore the kingdom. We must not forget to pray or remind others to pray for Jerusalem (Ps. 122:6). Our own lives are blessed as we love His people and pray for them.

The "mountain peak" experience came the morning we sat to have a picture taken on the Mt. of Olives overlooking Jerusalem. As I saw the gate (still sealed) in the background, I pictured Christ's feet touching down on that very mountain, just outside the city where He was rejected. I imagined the procession beginning in which He will enter the city to be received as King of kings and Lord of lords, the Messiah.

If sincerity alone was sufficient, the Jews would surely receive that for which they are praying. I have seldom witnessed such fervency in prayer. The tears we saw at the wailing wall and at David's tomb represent what the Jewish people long for, the peace of Jerusalem. As I thought about it later, I realized that their prayers are for earthly blessing on their nation. God must wait to answer those prayers until they receive His Son as He comes from heaven with spiritual peace.

The thrill of being in God's chosen land was moving. Yet even greater was the joy of seeing what God is doing in the lives of the saints in Japan. The combination of visiting Israel with a member of my family and seeing again what God is doing in Japan, certainly made our journey the trip of a lifetime. But the greatest impression of all was the greatness and goodness of the God we serve.

3
SO THIS IS MISSIONARY LIFE!

Gifford and I were in our mid-twenties when we arrived in China with our four-month old baby, Ruth. I still thank God for the shelter of the China Inland Mission home which provided a cushion in our adjustment from life in the United States to that of China. Nothing could have prepared us for the challenges of daily life in post-war China. Our little room at the home was a haven from the noise of the millions of people in the streets and shops. It provided a respite from the confusion and tension of dealing with government officials. How we needed that support!

We had expected to breeze through customs and be on our way to the mission station where they were waiting for us. But that was not to be. The customs procedure alone took two weeks. (We think the officials were waiting to receive bribes from us before they let us through.) Our booking on the riverboat was already set, so Ruth and I had to proceed inland without Gifford, who remained behind to cope with the custom officials.

One example of the delays Gifford experienced was being told to count the paper clips in an opened box. The box had been listed on the invoice but not the number of clips it still contained. Can you picture a young, energetic missionary, not too long out of military service and full of zeal for the Lord, sitting in a customs warehouse counting paper clips? Can you imagine him doing this while his wife and baby traveled into inland China without him?

Yet the delays brought blessings as well. One event that

23

happened while we were staying at the mission home is indelibly impressed on my mind. We were invited to the house of a dear British couple for afternoon tea. They wanted to get acquainted before we traveled further inland.

They were the model of warm, loving hospitality. They openly expressed great joy at the arrival of young missionaries to join the ranks. The welcome and love still warms me when I remember them. I was shocked, however, when I saw the circumstances under which this couple lived. Having had some interesting conversations with veteran missionaries, I was prepared to find difficult circumstances, but I still could not believe the actual living conditions. Their entire living quarters was smaller than the living room in my home had been. They had survived the war in a place with absolutely no modern comforts—no appliances, no window screens, no gadgets, and no glass. Not even rice paper covered the hole in the wall that served as their one window. But even though they faced the difficulties of many daily inconveniences, I have never met a happier couple in my life.

During our visit, the shutters of their one "window" were opened to give us a breath of air. We were thankful for the fresh air, but with it came a hoard of flies. Before long, one landed in Gifford's tea! Our hostess, with a great flourish and a big laugh, grabbed the cup of tea from his hand and ran to the window to scoop it out before it died. Then she handed the tea back to him because tea was expensive and a whole cup couldn't be wasted. We tried to share her happy spirit, but the whole incident was rather disconcerting to a squeamish new mother. Interestingly enough, it bothered Gifford more than it did me. He found it difficult to finish his tea.

This story came to mind after I heard a message from Ecclesiastes 10:1: 1 *"Dead flies cause the ointment of the apothecary to send forth a stinking savor: so doth a little folly him that is in reputation for wisdom and honor."*

The speaker had emphasized Solomon's unique way of

telling us to get the flies out before they die and cause the ointment (or the tea) to stink. There is no question in my mind as to why our hostess had been so quick with the spoon on that afternoon so long ago. When flies land in food, it means trouble later. There are hygienic reasons for scooping out flies and doing so quickly. It is no different in our spiritual lives. The speaker did an excellent job of likening flies to the little sins that land and soon pollute our spiritual lives if we ignore them. God's spiritual laws of hygiene are just as sure as His physical laws of hygiene. Although we are horrified at the thought of a fly swimming in our tea and would refuse to drink it, we are often not aware of spiritual "flies" that contaminate our spirits. Yet if we don't deal with them quickly, if we permit them to stay, they soon make a stink. The speaker then listed a few of those flies but didn't get very far. So I've tried to identify a few more of these disgusting creatures that pollute our lives and cause a stench.

Everyone's flies are different. When I am honest, I realize that quite a few of them constantly land in my "cup of tea," so I must always have the spoon ready for use. Paul, in Ephesians 4:26, expresses the same thought when he writes that we are not to give place to the devil. Paul uses *anger* as an example. We may not be able to keep the fly of anger from diving in, but he reminds us how important it is to scoop it out before we go to bed at night. In the same vein, the author of Hebrews spoke of *bitterness*, warning that it needs to be removed before it defiles, not only ourselves, but others around us as well.

Criticism is another fly I have become more aware of lately. I soon notice the effect it has on my spirit if I permit it to remain unchecked. It rots and spoils my influence for good. Who wants to be around a foul-smelling person?

A few of the more easily recognized spiritual flies (at least we quickly recognize them in the lives of others) are *adulterous thoughts, bad-mouthing, covetousness, daydreaming, envy, foolish talk, greediness, hatred, impatience, jealousy, pride, suspicion of oth-*

25

ers, and *laziness.* I'll let you finish the list. The best answer to the problem is to keep the flies shooed away before they land, but once they dive in, they must be scooped out immediately before they cause problems.

Let's not allow these dreadful flies to settle in when it is so simple to flip them away. John says that through confession and cleansing of Christ's blood we can rid ourselves of them instantaneously (1 Jn. 1:7, 9). Since I've retired to our comfortable United States, I find I need to keep the spoon close at hand. Although our living conditions are not primitive, nor do we experience the same abundance of flies, the irritations of daily life are as plentiful as they were on the mission field.

4
ALONE WITH THE LORD

John chapter 4 records the beautiful story of a woman whose life was completely changed through a few minutes she spent with Jesus Christ. She had been on His heart from before the creation of the world, and He knew she had a deep thirst for life, a thirst that her many marriages had not been able to fulfill. So knowing her need He went out of His way one day to meet her. By arranging every circumstance and detail so they could be alone (though in full public view) at the right moment, Christ gave her a drink of the living water that springs up into everlasting life. Their meeting led to a lifelong and eternal friendship that has blessed millions of people since that day.

We see the tender heart of the Saviour in the way He gently started a conversation with her. He simply asked for a favor— a drink of water. He went from there to make her conscious of her desire to quench her spiritual thirst. After arousing her curiosity, He brought her to an awareness of God and explained that He had a gift to offer her—a drink of the living water that only He, the Son of God, could give her. He revealed to her His identity, as the promised Messiah. He said, *"If thou knowest...who it is that saith to thee, give Me to drink, thou wouldest have asked of Him, and He would have given thee...."*

By seeing for herself who He really was, she was changed. But before Christ gave her the water she longed for, He had to make her aware of the sin that dominated her life and drove her to the place in which she found herself. He did this by focussing directly on her problem—her sordid past. Her self-centered life and her consuming desire for fulfillment had caused her separation from God and created the emptiness and meaninglessness in her life. She needed more than just His human listening ear, she needed to see the root of the problem—sin. One look at her own heart through His holy eyes accomplished more than a lifetime of human sympathy or advice could ever have done.

I see no resistance or self-justification on her part as Christ brought up the difficult subject of her sin. She had no spirit such as Saul exhibited in 1 Samuel 15:29-30: *"I have sinned, yet..."* For the first time in her life she saw her sin for what it really was in God's eyes—a horrid evil that would cost the life of the Christ (Isa. 53:4-7).

She immediately raised the question of worship, and He responded by enlarging on it. Even before she fully understood the matter of salvation, He explained God's desire for worship. The subject of worship caught her attention, so He explained that it was not the place and manner of worship that mattered, but the object of worship that made it acceptable to God. This explanation satisfied her and she seemed to realize that there was a connection between the promised Messiah and the true worship of God. She caught His spirit when He said, *"I that speak unto thee am He."*

I can imagine how her eyes opened wide as the truth of what He said touched her heart. She was actually speaking in person to the Man who was the Messiah promised in the Old Testament! I love to ponder the awed pause that took place between the 26th and the 27th verses as the full truth of the meaning of the Messiah's presence before her sunk in. She recognized Him as the Saviour sent from heaven to save her from her sin, and she acknowledged her position before Him as a sinner. Jesus went on to teach her about true worship springing forth from both spirit and truth. Her heart moved in gratitude and love as the wonder of true worship gripped her soul. Truth without the Spirit of God can be warped and harsh, yet

28

spirit without the truth of God is misdirected and meaning-less. Her faith grasped the truth that He truly was who He said He was—the Messiah, the prophesied One who was perfectly human, yet wholly God—inspires me because I sometimes fear that my thoughts of worship and God's thoughts are as far apart as earth is from heaven.

After the issue of His identity was settled, nothing else mattered to her and, catching His spirit, she immediately began to tell her friends about Him. Forgetting the mundane things of life such as water pots and the shame she had once felt in His presence, she rushed to the men of the city and begged them to come meet Him for themselves. She longed for them to reach for the thirst-quenching water of life. Her witness was clear. *"Come,"* she said, *"See a Man who told me all things that ever I did. Is not this the Christ?"* (Jn. 4:29).

It was no coincidence that the disciples returned from their trip to town as the men made their way to meet Christ. As the man approached, Christ told His disciples to lift up their eyes and get busy in the harvest field. These men also needed to hear the message Jesus had just presented to the woman. I believe the conclusion of this story is written in the book of Acts, when the disciples collectively caught the meaning of worshiping in spirit and in truth. Their message continues to go out to this day: *"But the hour cometh, and now is, when the true worshippers shall worship the Father in spirit and in truth: for the Father seeketh such to worship Him"* (Jn. 4:23).

5
AN ACCIDENT?

One afternoon, one of our colleagues at the mission station in inland China noticed a small airplane overhead that was flying far too low. This caught his attention because there was no airport nearby so the plane could not possibly be coming in for a normal landing. He became concerned because the mission station was surrounded by dozens of cone-shaped hills and he knew of no level ground on which the plane could land. The sound of the engine operating erratically heightened his concern. That pilot is in trouble, he thought, and immediately dropped to his knees to pray for him. He didn't stay on his knees very long, however, because he was following the plane with his eyes.

With a prayer still on his lips, he ran to his truck and headed in the direction in which the pilot was evidently trying to make an emergency landing. It took him some time to locate the downed plane, but to his relief, the plane had made a miraculously safe landing. There was very little damage to either the plane or its two occupants, who were smiling in gratitude. They were obviously shaken, but they had few bruises. Our colleague was surprised and pleased when he saw that the pilot and his passenger were both foreigners. He invited them into his truck and after a prayer of thanksgiving started off for home. It didn't take long for them to discover that they were of kindred mind. The pilot explained that his was a charted mission plane, and he was flying a single missionary to her station.

This was indeed an occasion for celebration. There were

tears of thanksgiving as the missionaries congregated to meet their unexpected guests.

In the will and purpose of God, a single man was on that mission station. During the few days during which arrangements were made for a second plane to continue the young woman's journey, a spark of interest was kindled in the hearts of these two young missionaries. This was followed by correspondence, and in the course of time, a courtship led to their happy marriage.

Not long after this, our area of China was surrounded by Communist troops. We all received letters from our various embassies—American, Australian, English, and Canadian—with orders to leave China immediately. A plane was chartered to airlift us, and we were evacuated to Hong Kong from our station in Kweiyang, Kweichow, China. We were then led to go in different directions. Our family went to Taiwan and later to Japan where we settled permanently. Soon we became involved with our own work and gradually lost contact with the others.

One day, many years later, a Japanese Christian brother came to the home and asked if I had the address of any Christians living in Thailand. His company was sending him on a business trip, and he wanted very much to meet some believers that he could fellowship with while there. I looked in our missionary handbook, but found no one to whom I could introduce him. Disappointed, he left for his assignment in Thailand.

A few weeks later, a radiant and excited young man returned to Japan and knocked at my door again. His eyes were aglow, and he was so full of his unusual story that he could hardly wait to tell me the details. He recounted that one noon he found himself at a luncheon in Thailand and sat across the table from a middle-aged couple. With the zeal of a young believer and led by the uncanny affinity of Christians for one another, he started a conversation with them.

Even with the handicap of language, the three of them soon discovered that they had their faith in the Lord Jesus in common. There was an immediate bond between them.

After introducing themselves as missionaries, the couple asked the young man how he had become a Christian. He gladly told them that he had met a missionary by the name of Gifford Beckon at a Bible class at his university. At the mention of Gifford's name, the air became charged and the couple found it difficult to maintain their dignity. Hands flew across the table for a warm handshake as they wondered at the marvel of meeting each other unexpectedly in Thailand. They were the couple who met each other after the airplane accident at our mission station in China!

Three people from different countries found themselves becoming bound together in the Lord through their mutual friendship with another missionary from yet another country. Through God's mysterious ways, individuals who had been halfway around the world were brought together without even as much as a proper introduction! An airplane accident in China decades before and a Japanese company that sent an employee to Thailand were masterfully coordinated to make this meeting possible. It was a faith-strengthening experience for this younger believer to meet his brother and sister in Christ in such an unusual manner.

"O, the depth of the riches, both of the wisdom and knowledge of God!...and His ways past finding out" (Rom. 11:33-36).

6
IT'S SO DAILY

Have you thought that our Christian walk would be so much easier if it weren't quite so daily? I remember having such thoughts. One night I returned home to face the daily stack of dishes and prayed, "Lord, I would be a much better witness for You if I just didn't have to come home night after night to these dirty dishes in the sink. If I didn't have to spend so much time here, I could be doing more profitable things for You." The Lord's response was quite different from what I expected. Instead of sympathizing with me, He reminded me that He knew how much time the mundane things of life required. Not only that, He brought to my mind how He had actually planned it that way so that His rebellious creatures wouldn't have so much idle time to get into mischief.

An advertisement I'd seen years before flashed through my mind. It pictured a stack of dirty dishes reaching to the ceiling. The caption read: "How many dishes do you do in a day? In a week? In a year?" I didn't expect a magic genie sent from heaven to scrape the dishes, wash them, and put them all away without physical labor, but I did tell the Lord I would much rather be out doing something for Him like visitation or teaching Bible classes. Washing so many dishes every night seemed like a big waste of time. The mountain of dishes in the advertisement reminded me that the Lord was counting every single rice bowl and Japanese tea cup! If I did my work for Him, knowing it was what He wanted me to do at the time, I would be as well rewarded for washing dishes as for teaching.

As much as we may discount it, our Lord places great value

on our daily service for Him. When Christ challenged His disciples in Luke 9:23-25, for example, He indicated that the labors of the Christian life would be a daily thing: *"And He said to them all, if any man will come after Me, let him deny himself, and take up his cross daily, and follow Me…For whosoever will lose his life for My sake, the same shall save it. For what is a man profited if he gain the whole world, and lose himself, or be cast away?"*

Christ's challenge helped me to visualize my problem with washing dishes as being my discipline at that particular time. My will was crossing God's will in the daily struggles of life. I was trying to pick and choose my service for Him according to my own liking. Something more glamorous than dirty dishes appealed to me, but His plan was for me to support my husband's evangelism and minister to my family for Him.

Yet by entertaining (and cleaning up after) the unsaved young people my husband brought home after Bible classes every day, I joined my husband in serving the Lord. We worked together as a team. God wasn't being unfair to me. He could look ahead and see what I now see when I look at photos taken at that time. Most of the faces of those Japanese young people I now recognize as the present-day elders and wives of elders in various Japanese churches. My role in God's plan, although it wasn't quite to my liking at the time, paid the biggest dividends by far and brings the most joy today.

I have also learned that there is no substitute for daily service. My granddaughter acquired her college education through a scholarship in cross-country running. She had to run daily. If she took a few days off, she felt its toll immediately. So she faithfully ran her miles every single day in order to keep in shape for the big races.

Just as there are days when we would prefer to set aside our service to the Lord, I know there were many days when my granddaughter would rather have slept in and skipped the early morning runs than beating it out step by step. But her persistence in running paid off by allowing her to earn her degree which qualified her to teach high school.

We also must choose to do our daily tasks faithfully. Christ instructed His disciples to daily take up the cross and follow Him. Joshua challenged his followers to do the same thing (Josh. 24:15): *"Choose you this day whom ye will serve."*

This means we must make our choice every day. Will I or won't I? Notice that Joshua said they must choose *whom* to serve, not *what* or *how*. Lest you assume that I think active service for Christ is the only way to get involved, let me hasten to say some of my greatest struggles are trying to live a righteous life in a sin-laden world. My natural thoughts constantly cross against God's desires for me. It takes a conscious effort to choose to bring my thoughts under the leadership of Christ. It is not easy to carry out this decision daily, but necessary if we are to live in harmony with Him.

We understand why the Lord admonishes us to choose Him as a daily exercise when we consider the devastation that results from even a little slip. Many lives have "gone down the drain" in the aftermath of a hasty wrong choice brought on by a lack of seeking the Lord's instruction. We see many examples of this in modern life as well as in the Scriptures themselves. Moses was a classic example of a man who faced a decision that was contrary to human logic. Gratitude for one's family is a virtue under most circumstances, but in Moses' case it meant a compromise with wrong living to stay in the palace. It is unlikely he could have chosen to leave the comforts of the palace and the love of his adoptive mother if he had not been making daily choices to follow God.

As we go through life, we can expect to face testing in seeking to serve God daily. Gifford, for example, was faced with a different choice at one stage in his prolonged illness. Although we witnessed miraculous healings in Japan, he made a choice not to go to a healing meeting. At the time, he was suffering untold agony. The nights seemed so long we often wondered how we would ever get through them. Meanwhile, large healing meetings were taking place in Tokyo and miracles were being broadcast all over Japan. In addition to our own personal desires to have complete healing for my husband, or at least freedom from the pain, three young brethren were urging us to attend meetings in Tokyo that were conducted by a famous woman healer. Their argument was a strong one. They said that many people would be brought to Christ if God were to heal Gifford miraculously. They tried to persuade us that he was such a valuable servant of the Lord whose testimony to the power of God would be far reaching, that we must seek healing through these meetings. Frankly, we gave it much thought and even much more prayer.

My husband made the choice not to go, however, saying that if God wanted to heal him, He could do it right in our own home. He reasoned that if God could save a soul apart from a big crusade, He could heal at home in the same way. He did not have to attend a meeting to be healed any more than an individual had to attend an evangelistic campaign to be saved. During the following months we both proved that the message of the cross of Christ was the power for daily living—and for dying (1 Cor. 1:18).

Gifford's decision was confirmed some months after he passed away. The three men stood before the congregation one Sunday morning and apologized for the discord they had caused over the healing issue. There were very few dry eyes during the morning service as the assembly again experienced harmony, peace, and unity. Today the growing churches in the area stand as witnesses to the daily miracles Christ brings about by continually proving His grace to be sufficient. He does use us as humans, but He is not limited to using only certain people.

I was tested again regarding the same issue within weeks after Gifford's death. I attended an evangelistic service in which a Japanese evangelist told the story of his miraculous healing. He had been in the hospital with advanced tuberculosis. From his hospital bed, he heard the gospel message over the radio and his heart was touched. He began corresponding with the speaker and a friendship formed between them. Believers from a nearby assembly started visiting him. His salvation soon followed and He grew quickly in the Lord.

One day he announced to his visitors he wanted to be baptized. There was a long discussion as to whether or not this should be done and how. Apparently his life was at risk. It was finally decided that a special plastic pool would be brought into his room and a date was set for his baptism. On the designated day, he gave a clear testimony before many witnesses (including hospital staff) of his faith in the one, true, living God. When it was time for him to be lifted out of bed and into the pool, he suddenly sat up, threw the covers back and put his feet over the side of the bed. Everyone in the room, especially his wife who was a doctor, showed total amazement when he rose to his feet without support. He later laughed as he repeated her exclamation, "You are so tall!" It had been a long time since she had seen him on his feet. He was soon released from the hospital and never was a bed patient again.

It was very difficult for me to understand what God was doing after hearing this story. His testimony sent me into a tailspin spiritually. I went home to one more sleepless night as I wrestled with the seeming unfairness of God. Why had the Lord healed this Japanese brother and taken my husband? It was only after I submitted to God's will and admitted to myself that God had the right to heal one person and take another home to be with Himself that I found peace. My husband had made the decision not to go to Tokyo for healing and I had agreed with him. Our brother had never once asked for healing and God gave it to him. The choice is God's.

The apostle Paul, too, had some difficulty handling the daily nature of his walk with God. Relief came when he acknowledged that the same Person who brought salvation in the first place, brings daily power through the message of the cross. He was under no condemnation for his sin, since Christ had paid for it all. He could say, *"Who shall deliver me from the body of death? I thank God through Jesus Christ our Lord."* God loves us to the extent that He wants to give us His life through the cross in order to keep us in fellowship with Him. This is done only when we take up our own crosses daily and choose to follow Him.

7
BLESS US WITH DEFEAT

During a routine trek through my neighborhood, I recalled the prayer of a missionary friend, a prayer that had been offered nearly fifty years before. Despite the passage of time, one sentence in that prayer still stands out. It was the request, "Bless us with defeat." I ought to explain the circumstances.

One hot afternoon in China, a missionary we had never met gave us a surprise visit. After introducing himself, he explained that he was traveling with a team that was conducting large evangelistic crusades in the interior of China. Somewhere along the way, he had been told that he just "had to meet" a missionary couple who lived nearby. So, on a free day between meetings, he came to see us.

Gifford was out at the time, and our guest asked me if I had a room in which he could relax while waiting for him to return. Even though it was a bare room with no furniture, it made no difference to him. He made himself comfortable on the floor and I left to make tea.

A short time later, I knocked, and poked my head in to find him completely occupied. The expression of joy on his face impressed me so much that I can still picture it today. He was sitting on the floor with his back against the wall, memorizing the 139th Psalm. When he saw me, with the biggest smile on his face, he said, "Listen to this: *'How precious also are Thy thoughts unto me, O God! How great is the sum of them!'*"

I could sense he felt deeply about this verse. He was reveling in God's goodness, rejoicing in God's compassion, and truly enjoying the Lord. He began sharing thoughts of the

Lord's great love even before I set the tea tray down before him.

I must have brought a snack with the tea and the occasion called for prayer. He bowed his head in thanksgiving for the refreshment and then prayed for the special meetings they were having. He closed with the statement, "If...Lord, then bless us with defeat." I was caught off guard by this strange request. How could defeat in gospel meetings bring God's blessing? How could God be glorified through a failure? That God would ever want to purposefully bring defeat in the preaching of the gospel was an entirely new concept to me.

It wasn't until a few years later when we visited this missionary and his family in Japan that I realized what a humble man he was and why he asked God to give him defeat rather than to allow him to think too highly of himself. Upon hearing his testimony, we learned the cause of his great joy in the Lord and his fear of bringing attention to himself.

This dear brother had been brought up in the Bronx, New York, under unbelievably difficult circumstances. His life at home had been horrid, but he found Christ in the midst of the struggle. He marveled at the fact that God had His eye on him even when he was a boy. He knew that God loved him the way he was, a dirty little boy from the wrong side of the tracks. He could not fathom why God had reached out to him through an invitation to a Sunday school class, saved him, and given him the privilege of serving Him.

This man's gratefulness and appreciation of the Lord made me envious. He never lost the wonder of his salvation, nor was any price too great to pay for being included in Christ's family forever. Psalm 113:7 and 8 was clearly demonstrated in his life: *"He raiseth up the poor out of the dust, and lifteth the needy out of the dunghill that he may set him with princes, even with the princes of his people."*

Because this man knew that he had been set with princes, he was extremely careful not to be tempted to become self-sufficient, prideful, or taking personal credit for God's work. He was willing to sacrifice his own success for the sake of Christ, even asking God to bless him with defeat if there was any possibility of it coming between him and his Lord. He had learned that God works more through a man's humble attitude than through His mighty deeds. He knew the difference between the wisdom and success that comes from above and brings peace and that which is earthly and causes envy and strife (see Jas. 3:13-18). He would have found that failure was sweeter to his soul than pride. He recognized the need to commit God's blessings back to Him in order to maintain a grateful attitude. His one consuming passion was to magnify the Lord. It inspired in me a fresh desire to bring God into clearer view through the magnifying glass of His Word.

I now know that his joy that long-ago afternoon in China came from his being able and willing to suffer failure. The remembrance of his passion for the Lord puts that same joy within my reach. To be kept from being prideful and taking credit to myself, it challenges me to have the courage to pray, "Lord, bless me with defeat."

8
ONE MORE THING

Eve had everything—a perfectly healthy, beautiful body that any teenage girl would envy, and a husband who was in perfect health, too. The two of them worked together at their own pace, without stress, and with a degree of harmony such as none of us have ever experienced. Eve had it all together and had nothing to desire until Satan dangled a bit of information in front of her. Disguising himself, he appeared to Eve in the form of a beautiful, sleek, colorful creature (Gen. 3:1-6). Once he gained her attention, the victory was won. Millenniums later, he still uses these methods successfully.

Satan suggested that Eve needed something more to be perfectly happy and content. He implied that she was too dependent on God and would have a much more exciting life if she had her independence. He indicated that a special formula in the fruit of the tree of the knowledge of good and evil would enhance her happiness and make her more intelligent. He implied that God knew something she didn't, and that He was keeping if from her because He didn't want her to become like Him. He also inferred that God was a liar. Satan dared her to test God to see if she would really die as God had said she would. Eve fell for it hook, line, and sinker.

I recognize this tactic because Satan is still using it today. He enticed Eve to reach out and take the fruit to bring her happiness without God's interference. Likewise, many people today are striving to become gods (either in this life or in the "hereafter") and to be able to control their own lives. Don't all of the false religions of the world begin with this same feeling—

contemplating their own answers to the question of life instead of looking to the Source of truth?

Eve had the best of everything—a good husband, a happy home, enjoyable occupation, and fellowship with God Himself in the Garden of Eden. Still, she wanted one more thing—to become *"wise in her own conceits."* If she had just a bit more special knowledge, then she'd have it made. So, taking Satan's advice, she reached out for the forbidden fruit.

Are we any better today? Don't we also find ourselves wanting better pay, fewer hours, one more room on the house, a better car, another friend, a more compassionate husband, or more perfect kids? You name it, Satan dangles it temptingly before us. Most of us think we deserve much more in life. Like Eve, we believe that all we need to do is reach for it and make it ours, instead of seeking God first with our whole hearts.

I can't speak for you, but that has been my history. As much as I hate to admit it, overeating stems from the same problem. Even though I'm honestly not hungry at the time, I reach out for the second helping because it looks so good. This same principle was the subject of Paul's concern in 2 Corinthians 11:3: *"But I fear, lest by any means, as the serpent beguiled Eve through his subtilty so your minds should be corrupted from the simplicity that is in Christ."*

If we reach out for anything God has forbidden or restricted, we will lose it just as surely as Eve did.

Eve's next step after her disobedience was to reach out for fig leaves to cover her nakedness that resulted from her rebellion against God. People have been trying to cover their nakedness before God ever since. God slew animals, shed their blood, skinned them, and made clothes for Adam and Eve to wear. Only then could God be satisfied.

In my lifetime, I have met plenty of people who had it all together in my estimation. Some had more money than they knew what to do with, yet they wanted more. I've known extremely well-educated and clever people with encyclopedic minds who wanted more knowledge. I've seen people in good health consumed with searching for ways to stay in better health. Some were even willing to give their last dollar to do so. Yet no satisfaction can be found in any of these things when we seek them apart from God. These things may not be wrong in themselves, but if we seek them first (thinking they will meet our needs apart from God), they become sin.

Nobody is satisfied with anything for very long. I recently drove by a mall that looked absolutely wonderful to me when I came back from Japan on furlough twenty-five years ago. I'd never seen anything like it in my life. It is now being torn down to be replaced with something bigger and better. This has to be done to keep up with the desires of the public today.

We would do well to ask ourselves what we are reaching out for at this very moment. What is it we think would make us content instead of seeking God? Satan dangles before us every imaginable temptation to compete with God's best. Reaching out for something to eat was not Eve's most serious sin. It was taking what God had said not to take, in rebellion against Him.

We would have fewer problems with such temptations if we decided as David did in Psalm 101:3: *"I will set no wicked thing before mine eyes."* We are less likely to reach out for things we don't see. Our alternative is to make the choice David did in Psalm 16:8: *"I have set the Lord always before me; because He is at my right hand, I shall not be moved."*

There are great risks in reaching out for anything or anyone other than God. Job, for example, reached out for sympathy and comfort from friends, but he did not receive that for which he longed. Instead, he received their unfriendly, unsympathetic, and condemning advice. He became so discouraged that he questioned why he had been born. And we think we have our "ups" and "downs"! Few of us have ever experienced what he went through.

In the first chapter of Job, we see him accepting all that happened as from God's hand, bowing down and worshiping Him in the midst of tragedy. Job 2:10 would indicate that Job recognized God as his Creator who had the right to send evil as well as good. As his friends gathered and shared their ideas about God's reasons for his suffering, he took his eyes off the Lord and become absorbed with his miserable circumstances. The result was (as it always is when we concentrate on ourselves) depression to the point of cursing the day he was born.

Exactly at that point, God stepped in and lifted Job's eyes to the heavenly and eternal. When Job was able to see the Lord again as He really is—supreme, holy, loving, and powerful enough to rectify everything—he stopped his heroic efforts to justify himself. When Job reached out for God, he found that God had been there all the time. Job cried out in desperation, *"Wherefore I abhor myself and repent in dust and ashes,"* and God took over. We know the rest of the story.

The apostle Paul is a great example of one who reached out for God's best. Until the day of his conversion, he had reached for education, prestige, and God's approval in the Jewish religion. God stopped him in his tracks, and he realized that these things were only appealing as long as he was on this earth. He changed his focus and began reaching out for the eternal. He expressed the longing of his heart with ever-increasing intensity in Philippians 3:7-14: *"I press toward the mark for the prize of the high calling of God in Christ Jesus."*

Let's permit God to stop us in our tracks. Let Him ask us what our hands are reaching out for at this moment. What do we think will give us happiness more than fellowship with God Himself?

9
When All the Pieces Come Together

I heard many moving, personal testimonies when I went back to Japan in 1997-1998. It was awesome to hear what God has done among the believers since my last visit. Yet the following stands out as the most interesting because the grand finale occurred just shortly before we arrived. The people involved were still very excited at the outcome.

The first piece of the story fell into place approximately thirty years ago, when a student started attending one of Gifford's Bible classes. A helpful, quiet, well-mannered girl, she never lagged in her spiritual interest and growth. But her quietness bothered me because I felt something was troubling her, as this did not seem to be her basic personality. She came to our home after class every week to discuss all she had learned that day. It appeared to me that she was trying to find the answers to some deep questions.

As our friendship deepened, she gradually confided that there was a problem at home, which I had already suspected. I had come to that conclusion because she was reluctant to go home; a cloud seemed to settle over us when it was time to leave. Her father was a school principal and her mother had her own business. Neither parent came home until late in the evening, and when they did they brought their tensions with them. The friction between the parents hurt the girl deeply. Her father was accustomed to running the home as he did the school. The mother resented this and became involved in her own activities, but remained a lonely, confused person. Their daughter felt caught in the middle and found it difficult to be fair to her mother and father, both whom she loved dearly.

After accepting Christ as her Saviour, she developed a strong faith in God's ability to help solve the family problems. The Holy Spirit gave her the joy, peace, and grace of a far more mature Christian. She learned soon in her Christian experience that Christ was enough to satisfy the longing in her heart and she prayed faithfully for the same for her parents. She brought her burden of loneliness and family problems to the Lord and was able to leave them with Him.

The first evidence of God's work on her behalf was her parents' agreement for her baptism. Her family had thought of her as a good person before, but they were very impressed by the new-found peace, joy, and love that she expressed to them. It wasn't long before her two older sisters began to question her about her unusual love for the Lord and for them. Within ten years, both were saved and had married Christian men. Her faithful, sweet testimony to her mother built a friendship with her as well. She was able to reach her mother by showing sympathy and understanding of her mother's need for affection from her father without alienating him. She also found ways to show affection for her father and in so doing won his respect and admiration.

During this same time period, God introduced the other piece of the story. A male high school student started to come to one of Gifford's classes in another town and was saved. He was fifteen when we met him. He was quite sick with asthma at the time. Many times, while spending the night in our home, he would have an attack. His attacks were so severe that I could hear him gasping for breath from our upstairs bedroom. I remember praying over and over again, "Please, Lord, don't let him die in my house."

The young man's father had died as a result of saving the life of a three-year old girl who had fallen into a lake. In order to support her family, his mother had taken a job in Tokyo, which required a two-hour commute daily. Thus he spent many hours on his own, much of it in bed. He realized his complete dependence on the Lord for physical health and quickly developed spiritually.

To shorten the story, I'll just say that these two young people were a vital part of the church and camp work for several years. Each contributed in their respective ways, and they both had an unusual burden to see their parents saved. The Lord, in His goodness, led them to share their lives together.

Their engagement party, twenty-five years ago, is still a very vivid memory. The fact that their marriage was acceptable to their families is amazing. I can remember my surprise that the girl's unsaved parents would accept a believer into their family. His long history of severe illness was another big factor against him. Plus, there was a real gap in the financial status of the two families, which is a great consideration with arranged marriages in Japan. As a parent, I felt deeply for the girl's unsaved parents. I knew the disappointment they must have felt when their daughter married so contrary to their hopes and dreams. She was their third daughter to leave the family religion and establish Christian homes. I still marvel that they cooperated so graciously.

After the couple married, they united their efforts to pray for their parents and gave a good word of witness whenever they could. Her father retired and began to get involved in politics and at the local shrine. All this time, he remained adamant in his unbelief. The daughter encouraged her mother because she knew the ache she carried inside, and a strong bond grew between them. Within a few years, the young man's mother was saved, and not long after that the girl's mother was born again. As Paul said, she really became *"a new creature in Christ Jesus."*

At the time they were married, the couple had a burden to help in a newly established assembly and eventually concluded that the Lord was leading him to become a full-time evangelist.

The church was flourishing in a remarkable way and agreed that this leading was in the mind of the Lord, so they backed the couple up with a commendation. This Christian brother gave up a good position and stepped out in faith, trusting the Lord to support them. Surprisingly, even in this, the family didn't oppose him. Most amazing of all, his health improved tremendously.

Not too many years later, the church began to feel the need for a larger building. They mentioned this need to the girl's parents, and the father and son-in-law discussed the situation on various occasions. The father viewed it from a business perspective and the son from a burden for growth in the assembly. The result was a long-term lease that allowed the assembly to build a chapel on the father's farmland. Everyone was happy when the chapel was completed. Contrary to the Japanese custom of the oldest child inheriting the family homestead, another lot of the family property was made available next to the chapel for a new home for the couple. Although the daughter was the youngest child, this was done because she had taken a large responsibility for the care of her aging parents.

Some time before my last visit, the couple was startled one morning by cries from the mother. The father had fallen in the yard and couldn't move. He was taken to the hospital and, as they suspected, had suffered a stroke. His recovery required a long time of rehabilitation and care.

The father was showing much improvement in his mobility and was really doing well, so it was upsetting when the couple received a phone call from the hospital at six o'clock one morning asking them to come immediately. The nurse in charge assured them that there had been no change in the patient, but that he wanted very badly to talk to them. She explained that the father had been pestering her to call them since two o'clock that morning. He had absolutely insisted, but she saw no change in the patient and refused to call them in the middle of the night just to satisfy a "silly whim" of his.

His "silly whim" was to share with them the experience he had during the night. But he didn't have to tell them—it was written all over his face. He was saved! He radiantly told them of the conversation he had with the Lord that night. He had confessed his sins and shared his joy with them over God's forgiveness. The mother stood back in unbelief, but he called her to him. He took her by the hand and apologized before them all for being such a selfish, wretched husband all these years. Her reaction was that it was too good to be true, but it proved to be real! The changes in his life left no doubt as to the reality of his salvation.

The father later returned home and commuted for further therapy. The next pleasant surprise came when he told the family that he wanted to be baptized. His physical limitations caused some logistical problems, but he was carried into the tank to give public witness that he was crucified, buried, and risen with Christ. I imagine the angels in heaven shouted for joy as they witnessed this dear, crippled man proclaim his Christian faith to the world. Since that time, he has been a vital member of the assembly, and dearly loved by everyone.

The climax to the story came shortly before our last visit to Japan. Her father again called the family together for a conference. He said that he wanted to break the lease, and everyone held their breath, waiting for him to explain his action. He explained that instead of holding the lease, he wanted to give the property to the assembly. This involved a mind-boggling amount of money because it meant the property under the chapel and the parking lot, which is no small gift. Just imagine what a testimony and encouragement his decision was to the believers. Imagine what it meant to the Lord! I believe it was only the moving of God's Spirit that enabled the other daughters to agree to forfeit yet another part of their inheritance. It was no small sacrifice for them.

The most recent news I've received is that the father is now being asked to give his testimony in places other than his own local church. It is exhilarating to see the whole picture—how God has made something so beautiful from two lives that are completely dedicated to Him. Their prayer and mine continues to be that of David's: "*Oh, magnify the Lord with me, and let us exalt His name together*" (Ps. 34:3).

10
GRANDMA'S CONTRIBUTION

Four generations of our family had gathered together to celebrate Thanksgiving. It was our last time together before Mother passed away. She was sleeping much of the time in those days as she grew steadily weaker, but she had been lifted out of bed and into her electric lounge chair so that she could be with us. I remember how peaceful and happy she looked lying there listening to our conversation. Although she was not participating, none of us was worried about her. Every chair in the living room was occupied, and for those who didn't have chairs, the floor was fine. Family jokes were plentiful. Everyone was in great spirits as we reminisced about old times.

Suddenly we heard the motor of the chair start to hum, and we saw Mother push herself into a sitting position. Her expressive eyes proved that she was very wide awake and alert. A hush came over the room as all attention focused on her. We waited silently for the pronouncement she seemed ready to make.

Her very short speech brought us all back to the real purpose of our gathering—Thanksgiving Day. The gist of her little talk was how different things would have been for us if the Lord had not saved her and Dad. Although I have thought about what she said many times since that night, the only two words I can quote accurately are "drunken sot." The third generation in the room may have thought she was exaggerating because none of them could imagine Grandma having had a drinking problem, but I knew differently. Mother was lying there, knowing that she was drawing closer to the time when she would see her Lord. She was thanking God for what He had done and was compelled to remind us not to forget our debts to God as well.

I knew Mother in her pre-conversion days; I was the only one who remembered parties that lasted well into the night. People had to be helped to their cars and taken home because of their intoxicated state. I clearly remember at the age of five waking up to a commotion in the early hours of the morning. Looking out to see what was happening, I was just in time to watch the men in the crowd toss a woman into the back seat of a car as if she were a bag of wheat. Mother told me more than once that the drinks at the parties had been a tremendous temptation to her. She had always been a morally upright, good woman but she had one weakness: she loved her wine and traditional whiskey and raisins, especially at New Year's and at weddings.

Mother wanted us to know that the wonderful time we were having as a family was due to the fact that God had saved us all from such a life. She wanted us to thank the Lord afresh that Christ was in our home. She and Dad had followed the Lord and were able to bring all four of their children to a saving knowledge of Jesus Christ, giving us a wonderful, Christian heritage. She wanted to remind us once more of our blessed hope in Him. She didn't want us to forget to thank and praise Him on that special day for all He had done for our family.

I don't know how Grandma's one-minute speech affected anyone else in the room that night, but it had a profound and lasting effect on me. I have never forgotten it. In her extreme physical weakness, Mother spoke louder to me in those few seconds than she could have done in a thousand messages. On that day she was surrounded by a caring family, she was well provided for, and she was on her way to heaven with peace and contentment. Yet without God's intervention, it could have been so different. She could have been on the ash heap, but instead she was a glowing example of Isaiah 61:3: *"To give unto them beauty for ashes, the oil of joy for mourning, the garment of praise* [and thanksgiving] *for the spirit of heaviness; that they might be called trees of righteousness, the planting of the Lord, that He might be glorified."*

It's often the things we don't have, or the situations from which we've been spared, for which we should be the most thankful.

11
WAITING EXPECTANTLY

I know very well that my father loved me and that I was always on his heart. This was especially true at Christmas time. Before he sold his business, he was very generous with his gifts to us. He would secretly take me by the hand to the closet where the Christmas presents were hidden, and allow me to peek at the beautifully wrapped gifts. They were piled high, just waiting to be placed under the tree. He would never tell me what they contained, but I knew it was nearly as hard for him to wait to open them as it was for me. I can still see the look of expectancy on his face as my brother and I entered the living room on Christmas morning. By the time we finished opening our gifts, the floor was littered with wrapping paper torn to shreds among the toys and treats.

It's a long story, but within a few years the situation in our family changed. The depression hit the United States and we felt it because there were no reserves in the bank. Things went from bad to worse for our family financially. When I was eight, there were no trips to the closet for an early preview of the Christmas gifts. I repeatedly looked in all the corners, on shelves, and under the beds...but there was no sign of a single gift anywhere.

Mother and Dad collected boughs from the woods near our home to make Christmas wreaths, which they sold in our front yard. The money we earned bought food for our table and treats for the Christmas Eve service at church. My brother and I helped fill small bags with oranges and candy. These were given to everyone after the service. After the Christmas program, in which we all had special parts, my parents invited a group of Christians in for a time of singing and fellowship. I was glad for the opportunity because it meant hot chocolate, homemade cookies, and the special treat of an orange each.

In spite of the good time we had on Christmas Eve, I was not looking forward to Christmas morning. I was sure there would be no gifts for us. I stayed in my room until hunger pangs forced me downstairs. With dragging feet, I finally descended the stairs and my brother followed. To my surprise, both Mom and Dad stood in the living room with a wonderful look of expectancy. They had been waiting for us, their eyes glowing with happiness. Then I saw why they were so happy. In the middle of the floor, a display caught my eye. It was a whole kitchen—stove, sink and cupboards, made out of bright blue painted boxes!

I can't remember what my brother got, but I remember how fun it was to inspect my homemade gifts. Dad was his usual enthusiastic self as he showed me the tiny leather hinges that held the cupboard doors. There were even little wooden door knobs by which to open them. It was a masterpiece in my eyes! Dad was as pleased by my reaction as I was by his gift.

At the time I never questioned where he did all his work, but it must have been in the crawl space under the kitchen. I hated that dark, damp place where fruit and vegetables were stored, so he must have been pretty sure I would never look for presents there. He had collected cardboard boxes, cut and reinforced them with wooden frames, and painted them. He worked late into the night while I slept. All the while I fretted about not getting anything for Christmas, he was working on his special surprise. His joy overflowed as he showed me every detail. I remember Christmas that year as being the best!

About ten years later, my parents created another wonderful memory that demonstrated their love for me. Mom and Dad had worked together to celebrate the fact that things were looking up for us. Mother had recovered from a prolonged illness and was able to attend to the household again. I had returned to high school after dropping out for two years to care for Mom and my baby brother.

I stepped off the bus one afternoon and could see the two of them waiting on the porch. Since they seldom welcomed me home quite so warmly, I knew that something good was about to happen. They silently followed me into the house and into my room where I customarily put away my books. It didn't take long to discover what gave them so much joy. I had a completely transformed bedroom! They had redecorated it. It was beautiful! Mother had sewn new curtains and a matching ruffle around the old vanity table. Even in the midst of the beauty, what stands out in my mind today is the joy they felt from my reaction as we exchanged hugs.

Isaiah 64:4 brings back these memories and leads me to think about God's joy when He gives us the many things He has prepared for us: *"For since the beginning of the world men have not heard, nor perceived by the ear, neither hath the eye seen, O God, beside Thee, what He hath prepared for him who waiteth for Him."*

Through the years, I have travelled and seen some gorgeous scenery. I've been to concerts and enjoyed beautiful and soothing music. But none of these pleasures can begin to compare with what the Lord has prepared for those of us who believe. Christ told us that He is preparing a wonderful place for us in heaven. Join with me in imagining our Lord as He anticipates that wonderful morning when He presents us with it all! I don't think I'm stretching my imagination too far in picturing the joy of His countenance as we enter heaven. Even now, is He any less pleased to see our happiness in receiving the benefits He pours on us than my own father was?

Will what He has prepared be any less wonderful than cardboard box kitchens and new curtains with matching ruffles? After many hours of play, my kitchen disappeared in an incinerator. My new curtains faded and wore out. But what

Christ has prepared for us will never perish! Nor will we ever lose interest in it. The gifts our Heavenly Father has created for us are incorruptible, undefiled, and fade not away (1 Pet. 1:4-5). Our gift is reserved in heaven with our name on it.

The more I think about it, the harder it is to see why my pleasure should mean anything to God, but it does! He is waiting for us with a smile of expectancy, His eyes aglow. That image ought to fill our hearts with unspeakable joy.

12
UNLESS I BELIEVED...

After many years of missionary work, I personally know of very few churches that have prospered without paying a price. Often many of God's people have passed through long periods of suffering in order to see God's work develop. In fact, in every place that I have seen a work for Christ established, I am aware of someone who had paid a great personal price to see it happen. They have endured financial testing or physical hardships, sacrificed family relationships, or have been humiliated to some degree by their own limitations. Even so, the testimony of so many workers in Japan has been the same as David's: *"I had fainted unless I believed to see the goodness of the Lord in the land of the living"* (Ps. 27:13).

And Psalm 34:19, *"Many are the afflictions of the righteous; but the Lord delivereth him out of them all"* is true of the Lord's servants the world over.

To illustrate this, allow me to share a story about one faithful local church in Japan that was established through the physical suffering and weakness of one dear sister.

This woman has suffered most of her life from rheumatoid arthritis and lives in constant pain. Her story began when she went to Tokyo to learn a trade and there met a missionary family who invited her to join their small Bible class. Her health prevented her from following through with plans to learn a trade, but she was in Tokyo long enough to hear the gospel, believe it, and determine to follow Christ her Saviour.

The woman returned to her hometown in the country a lonely, sick, discouraged woman, but she refused to stay that way for long. Her stiff body movements restricted her from being able to do most daily activities, but the doctor said that she would soon lose her mobility entirely if she did not keep walking. So she decided to shuffle into town every day to buy a few groceries. The walk, which for a normal person took about ten minutes, took her nearly an hour. The daily trips took all of her meager energy.

One day, a kindhearted, elderly woman who had noticed her daily trips called out to her to please stop for a minute to catch her breath. She gratefully accepted and rested on the porch for a time. Wiping the perspiration from her face, she drank the glass of cold water the woman offered to her. Before long, this break on her trips into town became a daily occurrence, and a friendship developed between the two ladies. It did not take long for the elderly lady to notice the radiance and positiveness about this dear sister. She could move two members of her body freely without pain—her tongue and her eyes—and she used both to great advantage. The first time I, as well as many others, met her, I was drawn to her happy face and sparkling eyes.

When the elderly woman asked the Christian woman about her unusually accepting and happy attitude toward her illness, the Christian shared her faith in the Lord with her newfound friend. She told her about Christ who had shared her burden and lightened it. Her contented face and bright eyes softened the sting of the truth about sin and the need of forgiveness before God. These daily visits soon turned into a Bible study, and before long, the elderly lady accepted the Lord as her Saviour and Friend.

The Bible studies began to grow as the elderly woman's family members became interested. After her daughter and daughter-in-law were saved, they developed a burden for the elderly woman's grandchildren and other youngsters in the neighborhood. They set aside a time every week to gather the children in to hear Bible stories and sing songs. By God's providence, an announcement concerning our Christian youth camp was given to these ladies, so they arranged for a group of children to attend.

We were completely taken by surprise when the ladies and the children (thirty-five of them) suddenly appeared in the middle of camp. I well remember my nervous reaction, for this doubled the attendance (and the work!). Although the counselors were all happy to see them, it put more pressure on them as well. We called an unscheduled staff meeting and decided that no one was to be turned away. Every single one of these children was a soul who was a future prospect for heaven. The dining room became a boy's dorm at night, and space was found to accommodate everyone. We laid straw mats on the tables and put benches together in the chapel for beds. (Although these measures would not be permitted by law today, they met the need at the time.)

When camp ended, the two sisters asked if they could all stay through the weekend and attend the next week's camp. When I heard that, I went into shock! Their request would require cooking for extra people over the weekend instead of taking a break, but after a time of earnest prayer I was willing to agree with Gifford and the other staff members to let them stay. As it turned out, all went well. I had plenty of volunteer help in the kitchen, and the ladies left camp at the end of the second week with double the enthusiasm to continue the Bible classes and work with children.

The ladies were like sponges when it came to absorbing spiritual truth, so other women gradually joined them. On special occasions, when a missionary or evangelist would visit, a few women brought their husbands to hear the messages as well. The missionary couple who had led the arthritic woman to the Lord continued making trips from Tokyo to help them. Another missionary couple from a neighboring city also came to help on a regular basis. The group grew steadily, and it became evident that an assembly was being formed.

As is so often the case when God begins to bless, Satan tries, in one form or another, to hinder the work by discouragement. So when the nucleus was being formed, persecution of these new believers began. One Christian lady who was newly saved, for example, was severely challenged in her faith by her husband. He took her to the river one night and in a drunken rage, threw her in. He hoped that the soaking would cause her to reconsider and give up her "new religion." She didn't relinquish her faith in Christ, however, and when her husband saw that she still loved him and prepared his meals as if nothing out of the ordinary had happened, he began to be willing to listen to the gospel.

Not long after this, the Lord laid this gathering of faithful believers and their unsaved friends on the heart of a Japanese evangelist. The Lord moved his family into the area to solidify the work. The assembly there has grown steadily ever since.

Although I could go on, retelling forty years of the history of this one assembly, I must bring this story to an end. Five years ago, at the dedication of the relocated camp, I was blessed to sit across the aisle from the man who had thrown his wife in the river. She sat beside him, and out of the corner of my eye, I saw them smile at each other during the service. Tears of joy overcame me as I remembered how God had brought this all about through a crippled woman and an elderly friend. That brother is now an elder in the assembly, and he supports the ministry of the new camp.

The dedication of the new camp was also attended by the crippled sister who was the beginning of the story and her elderly friend who is now a great-grandmother many times over. Both depend on Christian friends to help them get around now. I thought of the emotional and physical pain, and the long years of hard work that had been required to bear the fruit I saw that day. I witnessed the loving affection and care that was showered on these two women. They have lived to see the goodness of the Lord in the land of the living because they believed in the faithfulness of God. I praise the Lord that He has proved Himself worthy of such trust. He has rewarded them and will continue to do so throughout eternity.

"Unless thy law had been my delights, I should then have perished in mine affliction" (Ps. 119:92).

13
Longsuffering and Forgiveness

This getting old is for the birds! For me, over and above the usual body aches and pains, memory loss has been the most painful. Even in that, however, it isn't all bad. But one day I pulled a blunder that I thought my daughter would never be able to forgive. Thankfully, she did forgive me. The incident has brought new meaning to the necessity of longsuffering and complete forgiveness.

During the week before Christmas, I had managed to work in a lunch date with two of my daughters during my second daughter's noon break. We had a lovely time together and were on our way home when my youngest daughter asked me to let her off at King Soopers, a supermarket, to pick up an item she had forgotten to buy earlier. She was having a get-together and was already under a lot of pressure to prepare for it, so I was more than happy to help her out. I agreed to be back in about fifteen minutes to pick her up. After letting her off, I drove my second daughter back to work. Then I drove straight home instead of picking up my daughter as I had promised. About an hour later, I received a phone call. My daughter, in a pitiful voice said, "Mother, where are you?" I could hear the worry in her voice.

I replied, "I'm home, why? Where are you?"

"I'm at King Soopers!" came her shocked reply. She found it even more unbelievable that I didn't remember at which store I had left her.

It was only then that the truth hit home. Within fifteen minutes, I had forgotten my promise to pick her up. She was standing outside waiting for me in the bitter cold. Needless to say, I hurried to get her home as soon as possible. I felt terrible! I was sure she would never forgive me but she not only readily forgave me, she didn't even sulk or hold a grudge against me, which she could very easily have done. Rather, she showed concern for me.

I'm so thankful the Lord doesn't hold grudges against us. We have all been around people who just can't seem to forgive and forget an offense. It's a terrible feeling to ask for forgiveness and be told that you are forgiven, yet to see in the person's face that the cloud still blocks out the sun, the tension has never been released. It's awful to know that someone is hanging onto a grudge in their hearts because of some careless action that they think proves you don't love them.

In my case, my daughter readily and completely forgave me. However, the incident bothered me all afternoon because I knew the real cause of my forgetfulness. After dropping my daughter off at work, my mind had switched gears and I became deeply involved in trying to solve a problem. A previous conversation had completely filled my mind and had taken on such proportions that I'd forgotten everything else. My daughter had been standing out in the cold for an hour waiting for me because I had been self-occupied with a petty issue. I felt very small after identifying this as the reason for my failure to pick up my daughter. Yet, she had forgiven me without any hesitation, just the same.

I found myself wondering how many times I had stood Christ up, keeping Him waiting (out in the cold) because I had other guests in my mind with whom I was more occupied at the time. Sometimes, without really meaning to, I've made other people more important than Christ. I've allowed other matters to take priority. You would be shocked if you knew some of the unworthy thoughts I've had of the Lord when things didn't go just as I had imagined they should. It's a wonder He ever forgave me for the Cross, and it's an ongoing wonder to me that He freely keeps on forgiving me.

I recall one afternoon in particular when I was frustrated by a sudden turn of events. I'd been through a long, drawn-out period when things went from bad to worse. Then, just when things had begun to look up, the rug was pulled out from under me without warning. I didn't understand how the Lord was working, nor could I see any reason for my up-and-down circumstances. I had even thanked Him for the improvement when suddenly everything unexpectedly went topsy-turvy again. I now see how my desire for improved circumstances had become more important to me than focusing on Christ.

During Gifford's long illness, I was tempted to wonder if the Lord was playing a game of cat and mouse with me. There were several times after surgery when it looked as if the Lord had healed him. Then he went down worse than he had ever been before, until finally God took him home. I realized the seriousness of my sin before God as I saw the truth of what I was doing. I was not letting God be God in my life. I had momentarily lost sight of the holiness of God and put Him down on my level. I needed a reminder that He had made me, and had the right to do with me as He saw best—even when it did not in any way match up to what I saw as good for me.

In Romans 5, we learn that Christ not only forgives our human weaknesses, He also forgives our outright sin against Him. I had been reaching out for what I thought would bring satisfaction to me. But God forgave me even when I became His enemy through my rebellion at His authority. I realized how unworthy I was in my reactions to what God was working out in my life for my good. I was appalled to realize that I had actually put myself in the place of judging Him!

How must Mary of Bethany felt when she anointed the feet of Jesus with her ointment and wiped them with her hair (Jn. 12:1-8)? At that moment, surely she was appreciative of His longsuffering in forgiving her sins. Her position at the time was one that kept her from looking at anyone else in the room.

She was conscious only of herself as a sinner and of Him as her Saviour. Mary had truly learned to worship and bow down before Him in reverent awe. She knew who He really was, and what He meant to her as she listened to Him speak at her house (Lk. 10:38-42).

Mary was thankful for what Christ was about to do on her behalf at the Cross. She saw Him as ointment poured out for her. Solomon expressed the same sentiment in His special little book, the Song of Songs which is Solomon's. In verse 3 of chapter 1 he says, *"Because of the savor of thy good ointments thy name is as ointment poured forth, therefore do the virgins love thee."*

Many other people whose worship is recorded in the Scriptures also bowed down with their heads to the ground in worship. A good example of this is found in Psalms 95:1–99:9,

> *O, come let us sing unto the Lord: let us make a joyful noise to the Rock of our salvation…O come, let us worship and bow down: let us kneel before the Lord our Maker…Exalt ye the Lord our God, and worship at His footstool; for He is holy, …O Lord our God: Thou wast our God that forgavest them, though thou tookest vengeance of their inventions [at the cross] Exalt the Lord our God, and worship at His holy hill, for the Lord our God is holy.*

14
NOTHING WITHOUT CAUSE

On a quiet afternoon, I received a newspaper clipping from a cousin about my childhood church. Fortunately I could devour it word for word without interruption. It activated my long-term memory and flooded my mind with happy remembrances.

The minute I opened the letter I recognized a picture of the building immediately. The last time I had seen it was several years previously, and at that time I'd not been able to recognize it because it had been given a face-lift to match the surrounding new businesses. It had been turned into a saloon and much more. I had gone to see it with happy expectations of seeing the place again, but left with a very heavy heart. But I had a completely opposite reaction when I eagerly read the newspaper story: *"Volunteers...strip away the old and soiled...There were plenty of volunteers which helped complete the work faster than we anticipated. It was pretty impressive."*

Many details followed, telling about various companies and organizations that had donated time and money to strip away the old facade and reveal the beauty of the original edifice. The building was renovated to house an outreach ministry and has become a shelter where "physical, emotional and spiritual help will be offered to needy people." I praise the Lord that the building had been restored to its original purpose—to serve the Lord.

The picture of the church building in the center of the article fascinated me, and I let my mind wander back over the wonderful years of my childhood spent in that building. That had been the focus of our family's spiritual and social life for eight years. I was saved and baptized while attending there, and most of my memories were happy ones.

One memory resurfaced from the "not too happy" file, however. I had suffered much from a series of articles published in the local newspaper about my dad. The first article was about a fire that gutted the basement of the church. The caption read: HELL-FIRE PREACHING PREACHER STARTS FIRE IN CHURCH. Although they admitted the fire wasn't set intentionally, they didn't downplay the stupidity that had caused it. They had lots of fun at my father's expense. Looking back, I'm sure the whole experience was not intended to be hurtful. The reporter had an interesting article and wanted to make the most of it, but I took it personally. The effect it had in my life as I suffered the jeers of schoolmates and towns people I found unbearable. I was devastated.

The memories probably wouldn't have been so vivid had I not recently shared memories of those early days with my sister in Florida. She had reminded me of her version of the same story. Her elementary school was only a block or so away from the building, so when the fire trucks came and the word spread it was our church, her teacher excused her to see for herself what was going on. My high school was in another section of town, so I knew nothing about it until I returned home from school in the afternoon.

I learned more details the following morning from the newspaper article. My dad and a couple of other men were trying to repair a leaky roof when a tiny bit of tar they were heating spilled into one of the burners of the kerosene stove. The result of their carelessness was horrifying. The longer I meditated, the more I thought about the months and years that followed the fire. For the first time, I saw a chain of events that resulted from the attention the articles about the fire had been given in our town. Instead of the church fading out of existence as was predicted, it was actually "put on the map."

Attendance doubled, then tripled, as people became interested in this "hell-fire preaching preacher." They came to hear what he had to say that made him so infamous.

A doctor's wife was saved and asked to be baptized one Sunday night. Her husband threatened my dad, saying, "If that preacher socks my wife in the river I'm going to kill him." (Due to repairs on the church, the river became a substitute baptismal tank.) It was just an idle threat, but to me it was real. To hear my dear dad being made the brunt of so many town jokes was a difficult pill for me to take at the time. I carried fear in my heart for days before and after the baptism.

As I gradually began sorting out the events related to the fire, Ezekiel 14:23 took on new meaning: *"They shall comfort you, when ye see their ways and their doings: and ye shall know that I have not done without cause all that I have done in it, saith the Lord God."*

An amazing peace and comfort grew stronger in me the longer I meditated over the past and saw the Lord's Almighty hand in everything that had happened.

Dad did not stop preaching or change his message. The fire and the newspaper articles were a trial to my parents' faith, but God honored their trust in Him and their sincerity. My parents' faith was clearly seen by our family and our whole town as well. Yet it wasn't my parents' faith, but the *trial* of their faith that brought God's name before thousands of the newspaper-reading public.

First Peter 1:7 reminds us: *"The trial of your faith, being much more precious than of gold that perisheth, though it be tried with FIRE, might be found unto praise and honor and glory at the appearing of Jesus Christ."*

As a result of my parents' trial, many people were brought to the Lord for salvation. This thought alone brought great joy and a fresh appreciation for the wonderful working of God. Without doubt, the whole story will bring praise, honor, and glory when our Lord and Saviour, Jesus Christ appears.

As I reminisced, the face of a school teacher came before me. I realized that God had sent her into my life just at that time to help me through this difficult experience. Although she did not agree in the least with what my father was preaching from the pulpit, she did reach out to me as her student with a love I still remember. She went out of her way to encourage me by stopping me in the hallways to offer a little compliment on my clothes or something she had seen my mother wearing while she was shopping. She found many ways to help me see a positive side to life by praising both my mother and me. I remember she told me how dignified my mother always was at school functions. It made me feel so much better. God sent her into my life to encourage me to keep on in spite of the difficulties and misunderstandings. Today, these thoughts remind me that God always has someone to help in time of need.

With a heart full of gratitude, I began to praise the Lord for all He had done. First, I praised Him for the restoration of the old church building. It was beautiful again, and was being used for the Lord. Then I praised Him for my thoughtful, loving school teacher. I ended my little rendezvous with the Lord by thanking Him that He, indeed, had a reason for everything He permitted—no matter how traumatic it might seem at the time. I pray that the trials of my faith will bring praise, honor, and glory to the Lord at His appearing, too.

15
THE CHALLENGE OF HOPE

A ship that is permanently docked in Yokohama as a tourist attraction brings priceless memories to me. After one of our furloughs, we sailed back to Japan on that ship and were hit by a hurricane. For days the ship was tossed about like a cork. No matter how tightly we wedged ourselves into our bunks with pillows and blankets, we were thrown out on the floor. Each time the ship heeled to one side, we held our breath until it righted itself again. Even more frightening than the motion was the creaking and groaning of the ship. I fully expected it to break apart at any minute. We dozed off to sleep occasionally, but it was impossible to relax enough to sleep soundly. We became exhausted.

Several days into the hurricane, the engines stopped completely. The silence was equally as frightening as the roar of the storm. We realized we were without any power whatsoever. The captain had no way to maneuver the ship. We were stranded in waves that reached the height of the mast.

Gifford went out to seek information as to what had happened. He learned that a part of the shaft that connected the power to the rudder had snapped due to the extra pressure. A crew member told him they would have to make a new part right there in mid-ocean and replace it. When Gifford returned to our cabin, we talked over the situation. We were absolutely helpless until the ship's engines were running again. Literally, if the Lord didn't rescue us, we were sunk.

As we huddled together and prayed, completely putting our lives in the hands of the Lord, the sweetest sense of peace began to come over us. It wasn't long before we both fell into a deep, long sleep. Our circumstances had not changed, but our attitude had. When we awoke, we were thankful to still be alive and felt refreshed.

Even now, the thought of the hope we had in the Lord's ability to save us from the storm and the effect it had on us encourages me. Whether the storm abated or we drifted out of it, I can't even remember. What is important is the lesson we learned about the Lord's care and power to save us. That lesson still renews hope whenever I recall the incident.

The author of Hebrews summed up our hope better than I can explain. In Hebrews 6:19-20, he wrote: *"Which hope we have as an anchor of the soul, both sure and steadfast, and which entereth into that within the veil, whither the forerunner is for us entered, even Jesus, made an High Priest for ever after the order of Melchizedek."*

Christ is our anchor, our eternal security in heaven. He is not moved by the tide. He is safe and secure, where waves and wind cannot buffet Him. Christ has taken up His High Priestly work on our behalf, and has sent the Holy Spirit to be our help within. At the time of that frightening hurricane, we realized that we were just as safe as His disciples were when He physically climbed into the boat with them.

The deeper I delve into the subject of hope, the more I am challenged by the reality of it. When I first began writing about hope, I faced a pretty hopeless situation. Tears often came as I questioned whether I really believed what I was writing. Did I even know what hope was? The hope which the author of Hebrews wrote about, is a present confidence that the Lord Jesus Christ is our answer to our future. It is one thing to say we hope in God, but it is quite another to work it out in our daily lives. It is a real challenge to have hope when everything ahead looks black, and there is no visible basis for believing there is a solution.

The longer I wrote about hope, the more the memories of

the incident on the ship came to mind, and my sense of peace returned. My circumstances didn't change, but my attitude toward them did. Actually, one little word, the word "forever," in that portion of Scripture is what God used to renew my hope. (Not even one word in God's Book is superfluous!) On that desperate night in mid-ocean, I had been heartened by my husband's faith and hope; it had put me to sleep. Now the hope I need is something eternal and sure for myself because Gifford is no longer here for me to depend on.

I don't think any generation before us has been laden with so many hopeless people who face so many hopeless situations. I am constantly challenged by the need for answers to problems for which I have no answers. But I can look to Christ. I can point the person to Him as the only sure hope and trust. But each of us must follow through in seeking the hope God alone can give. We often don't want His answers. We want relief from our problems which is just as impossible as Gifford being able to stop the waves and the rocking of the ship.

None of us can live without hope. In a hopeless society, we need a strong sure hope for ourselves before we can reach out to others. So I ask you, what is your hope? What gets you out of bed every day? What is your security blanket? What do you look forward to today? Tomorrow? Next year? Twenty years down the road? We will never be good witnesses for Christ if we also are in a hopeless state of mind. In the same way that it takes a satisfied customer to speak convincingly for any product, we have to be absolutely certain of our hope in Christ.

Rebekah certainly needed hope when she made the tremendous decision to leave home and travel 1,500 miles with a complete stranger (Gen. 24:58). Every day as she got up to face another trying, hot, dusty ride on the trail, she had to make a new choice to keep going. There must have been times when the way seemed endless. It probably renewed her hope to glance now and then at the bracelets on her wrist. What kept her pressing on? It was her belief in what the servant had told her: a young man awaited her with the promise of every provision and the hope of a happy, fulfilling marriage.

In a similar way, the thoughts we have of our eternal Bridegroom can keep us steadfast when the way gets hot and dusty or the hurricanes of life hit. It helps us to look at the "earnest of our inheritance" revealed in His Word that remind us of the fullness of the blessing awaiting us. These promises give us courage and hope to press on. When we lack this ballast, we have lost sight of the truth that Christ is our hope.

There ought of be no such thing as a hopeless believer because hope is simply a matter of faith in the future tense. It is ongoing trust in the Man who died for us. I've had hundreds of hopes and dreams for myself, my family, and the church of Christ, but my hope cannot be in these things. Our circumstances change constantly and the things for which we hope fizzle out at times. Many of them never come to fruition. Hope that is wrapped up in people is often dashed to the ground.

Shattered hopes tempt us to think that there isn't much to live for, making it a chore to get up in the morning. I've personally lost hope countless times because I had hoped in things and lost sight of the fact that Christ is my hope. At such times I found that I had to make a decision to cleanse my spirit and renew my hope. Paul repeatedly told us to rejoice (find reason to go on hoping) in the Lord. If we look to Him, He will never let us down. He remains the same yesterday, today and forever.

Satan lives up to his reputation as our adversary, creating feelings of hopelessness and discouragement. All too often he succeeds by persuading us to believe his lies and to lose our hope. He distracts us by getting us caught up in activities that keep us from our Source of strength. Furthermore, his accusations against us as God's children are equally successful. He accuses us to ourselves, which causes us to become even more sensitive to the accusations of others. When we find this happening, we need to revive our hope through the blessed truth of Scripture. *"It is finished."* When we realize that He has per-fected forever all that concerns us because of the Cross, we can relax in His care. We find hope in Hebrews 10:14: *"For by one offering He hath perfected FOREVER them that are sanctified."*

Another of Satan's tricks that leads to hopelessness is to convince us that the temptation we face isn't all that bad if we should do it. "After all, everybody does it," he croons. "It won't hurt anyone. No one will even know." Then, after we capitulate to the temptation in question, he crushes us with guilt and makes us feel that there is no hope for us.

A young mother I knew was in this situation. She got her-self into the position in which she married an unsaved man. She told me that she let herself get involved because she thought God would forgive her anyway. She expected to appreciate the love of the Father far more after she strayed from Him. With bitter tears, she admitted that it didn't turn out the way she thought it would. Although she knew God had forgiven her, she was so crushed by guilt that she couldn't accept His forgiveness. For a time, she was convinced she was not even a believer. She felt completely forsaken by God and separated from His love.

What a joy it was to bring this dear straying lamb back to the assurance that is expressed in our verse in Hebrews. Christ is in heaven as our Great High Priest. He is sufficient for both our forgiveness and for enabling us to go on living—even with the consequences of our sin. As our hope, He gives us the peace to continue on in our Christian walk. The more we learn of Him through His Word and seek His forgiveness when we offend Him through unbelief, the more we will experience His joy, hope, and peace. This truth does not make us careless about sin, knowing how large-hearted is our heavenly Friend. Titus gave us the secret of present victory over sin and the enemy of despair when he writes of this hope in Titus 2:12-13: *"...Teaching us that, denying ungodliness and worldly lusts, we should live soberly, righteously, and godly, in this present world;*

looking for that blessed hope, and the glorious appearing of the great God and our Saviour Jesus Christ."

Holiness is a love relationship with our absent but soon-coming Bridegroom. It was the present joy of the future hope of meeting Isaac that kept Rebekah going!

16
GODLY SORROW

Can you imagine the remorse Peter felt when the Lord looked at him during His trial? (Lk. 22:60-61). What did Peter see in those eyes? Rebuke? Pity? Grief? Pain? Whatever it was, it triggered tears—a deluge of them.

While we were studying a portion in Mark 9 in our Japanese Bible class in Denver one evening, we witnessed a similar tearful reaction on the part of one of the Japanese sisters. She, too, suddenly began to weep—softly at first, and then without restraint. I knew she was in deep agony of soul, so I paused in the lesson to ask her if she wanted to talk about her grief. "I deserve to have a millstone hung around my neck and to be cast into the sea," she blurted out. She reread verse 42 to the astonished women: "*And whosoever shall offend one of these little ones that believe in Me, it is better for him that a millstone were hanged about his neck, and he were cast into the sea.*"

We were all amazed by her honesty. She went on to explain the reason for her self-assessment.

The woman felt responsible for causing her daughter to stumble because of her inconsistent Christian life. She revealed that she had attended an English Bible class as a high school student in Tokyo, believed the gospel, and was soon baptized. A few years later, she met a charming American soldier who persuaded her to marry him. Knowing that he was not a believer, she married him anyway and moved to the United States. I'd heard stories such as this before, but never with the conviction of sin that this woman was experiencing that night. The seriousness of her failure hit her full force as

)nted the reality of the consequences of living with
ieving husband as if she were not a Christian.

ughter was in the throes of getting a divorce and the
woman said, "It's all my fault; I failed the Lord!" and started
to cry again.

I said as gently but as plainly as I could, "It is true, you do
deserve to be thrown into the sea, but do you expect that the
Lord will do that to you?"

She stared at me for a minute or two while the meaning of
my question sunk in. I quickly added, "I deserve the same
treatment, but I don't expect to receive it." I then reminded her
that she would never be cast into the sea because Christ had
paid for her sins and had cast her sins into the sea. She could
put her trust in Him (Mic. 7:19). I went on to explain that I felt
I had caused my children to stumble by being inconsistent at
times, too. And I reminded her that, at the same time, her
adult daughter was responsible for her own actions. The
daughter had heard the gospel clearly many times. If she
feared God enough, she would choose to receive Christ for
herself, in spite of her mother's failures.

I've heard of many similar confessions from other parents,
including missionaries and Christian workers. Some felt they
had not given their children enough of their time. Others felt
they had caused their children to stumble by being examples
of compromise or worldliness, by failing to teach them proper
priorities. Although all of us deserve to have a millstone
around our necks and be cast into the sea, that will never happen to those who have been cleansed by the blood of Christ.
We are foolish if we allow ourselves to walk around carrying
a millstone of guilt. There isn't a single one of us who, on our
own merit, deserves to live. We have all failed God in one way
or another. We all fall short of His glory.

We who have truly placed our trust in the Saviour are
secure in our salvation through Christ's blood, but we are
freed from the burden of guilt through confession and forsak-

ing of our sin. The relief our dear sister evidenced was soon felt by the other ladies. The whole tone of the class changed as we went back to our lesson. She offered no light apology to Christ. Hers was a sincere confession of sin. Admittedly, repentance is a miserable experience, and we make the stubborn mistake of putting it off as long as we can. Yet repentance is absolutely necessary if we are to keep the joy of God's salvation and return to sweet fellowship with our Lord. ✗

Later, the same ladies and I addressed the subject of the difference between punishment for our sins and the consequences we reap because of them. If I neglect to water my garden and the vegetables don't grow, for example, that is a consequence, not a punishment. Christ bore the full punishment for our sins, but we often have to live with the terrible consequences of our sins. When I am slothful in spiritual things, I will reap spiritual weeds in the garden of my heart. Galatians 6:7-8 explains this well: *"Be not deceived; God is not mocked; for whatsoever a man soweth, that shall he also reap. For he that soweth to his flesh shall of the flesh reap corruption; but he that soweth to the Spirit shall of the Spirit reap life everlasting."*

Every time I confess a sin, it's like pulling another weed. We can thank God that He specializes in turning the curse of consequences into blessings.

In contrast to the lady who was so tenderhearted and cried so bitterly over her personal failures, was an unsaved lady who attended another class but would not admit that she had ever sinned. She appeared unable to see sin for what it really is in God's eyes. She had attended the class for at least two years and still declared her innocence. Other believers and I had tried to arouse her awareness of various sins that are so common to women such as jealousy, gossip, lying, grumbling, and so on, but she never grasped that she was guilty of anything called sin. She declared many times that she was not a sinner. She claimed to have always obeyed the gods and been faithful in her morning offering to the spirits of the ancestors.

She felt no guilt or accountability to the God of the Bible because she didn't believe He existed. I even arranged for a Japanese evangelist to speak with her, but she remained unconvinced. There was no outward evidence of the working of the Holy Spirit in her life.

One Sunday evening I felt a great burden for this dear lady. When I called to ask her if I could visit her, she offered a warm invitation to come that evening because her husband was working and she was alone. After about a two-hour conversation, I suddenly decided to go home. I had gotten nowhere. She always was ready to speak about the Bible, so I knew there was genuine interest, but no conviction of sin was evident. I shut my Bible, returned it to the case and said, "I must be leaving now; it is such a pity that Christ did not die for you."

With a shocked look, my hostess asked if that meant she could not be saved and would not go to the same heaven the rest of us looked forward to. I reminded her that it was impossible to enter heaven without the eternal life we receive in Christ Jesus. Then I added, "Christ only died for sinners, and according to you, you are not a sinner."

She looked so distressed that I sat down again and waited quietly while she sat thinking. After a very long pause, she looked up and asked, "Would your God, the God of your Bible think that leaving a husband and three children to marry another man was sin?" I assured her it was because He had forbidden such behavior.

She lowered her voice and said, "Then I'm a sinner." Without any outward sign of emotion or tears, she simply admitted to being a sinner. I asked her if she was willing to tell the Lord what she had just told me. She was more than willing to pray. I am sure she was born again that evening because her prayer revealed a fear of God and His ability to punish sin. The fact that she is now a believer is evident because her old ways have become new. She is always eager to present a clear message of salvation to new people who come to the class.

Although outward reactions differ, repentance always has the same inward effect—a changed life and the assurance of salvation. What a wonderful Saviour we have! What a marvelous salvation He gives!

"Now I rejoice, not that ye were made sorry, but that ye sorrowed to repentance; for ye were made sorry after a godly manner...for godly sorrow worketh repentance to salvation not to be repented of" (2 Cor. 7:9-10).

In other words, if we truly repent, we will never repent of repenting; we will never be sorry we were sorry!

17
SNIFFING DOGS

In some respects, we had much more freedom to preach the gospel in Japan than we do in our own country. As long as traffic was not hindered, we were free to conduct open air meetings and distribute literature. For this freedom, Gifford was most thankful. There was nothing he would rather do than go to the park in central Takasaki on Sunday afternoon and have a street meeting. He would take a group of people, and, using an old bandstand as a platform, would start speaking to the handful of listeners he had brought along in the micro-bus. Someone would play the accordion, and it was never long before a crowd began to gather.

One Sunday afternoon, from my vantage point in the front line of bystanders, I noticed a little fellow and his mother join the crowd. He was about two or three years old and was so cute I couldn't keep my eyes off him. At first he was really good and gave his mother no trouble. Gradually I noticed that he was getting fidgety and ventured farther and farther from her side. She was listening so intently that she didn't seem to notice him as he headed for the swings. As I saw him inch away, I began to move in his direction to keep my eye on him. I knew his mother was preoccupied, listening to the message of the gospel.

In a short time, he was quite away from the crowd and enjoying every minute of being on his own. He began laughing and skipping, basking in his freedom out from under his mother's thumb. Crawling up into one of the swings, he got himself swinging a little bit. What fun it was for him to be doing what he had come to the park to do! All was going well. To my surprise, his mother still didn't notice that he was gone. She was taken up with what the speaker was saying.

About ten minutes later, a huge dog, at least twice as large as the boy himself, lumbered over to the swings and started to lick some of the children. A few of the children seemed to like the attention of the dog, but when the dog came over to this little boy and started to sniff his legs, he let out one hearty scream. That was all it took. His shriek caught his mother's ear and she was there in a split second. Although other children were screaming too, she recognized her son's voice and reacted immediately to it. Her arms went around him as she wiped away the tears. He was safe! He had lost his freedom but didn't seem to mind. He settled right down, took her hand, and walked back to the circle, content because his mother was close by.

The incident I witnessed reminded me of so many Scriptures. Peter tells us that Satan goes around like a roaring lion, seeking whom he may devour. He does so when he sees us inching away from the Lord's protection. Although I usually think of God as Father, when I thought back to the little boy, Isaiah's description in which God claims to comfort as a mother (Isa. 66:13) came to mind. The mother's love and action was very touching. She comforted and loved her child and brought him back to her side.

As we read the Scriptures, we see many people who gradually inched away from God just as the little boy did. God, in His great wisdom, lets various dogs come and sniff around them. Most of the time they are only dogs, although some are larger and more frightening than others. Thank God that at the first sign of distress from us, He responds to our cry just as the mother did. God's goodness permits circumstance to frighten us and causes us to feel our need for His loving protection. He allows times of fright, and if we turn back to Him, they turn out for good in the end.

With my eyes fixed on the swings in life, I find myself inching away from my heavenly Father at times. After sixty years of experiencing the Lord's love, He still hears my cry whenever the dogs come sniffing around me. It is amazing how many dogs the Lord permits to lumber our way in order to bring our attention back to Himself. Although the fears are "legion," His comfort and love are instantly available, and He never fails to respond to us. Many times I have felt His love through a timely letter, phone call, tape, or radio message. But most often, He uses a portion of His Word to demonstrate His longsuffering toward His children: *"The Lord passed by before him, and proclaimed; the Lord, the Lord God, merciful and gracious, longsuffering, and abundant in goodness"* (Ex. 34:6).

18
ABUNDANT LIFE

I'm in a quandary. I have much to write concerning a delicate subject, but it is difficult to do so without betraying the confidence of the people involved. When I recently visited Japan, the Lord brought four people to my attention who have experienced a complete turnabout in their personal lives since I retired eleven years ago. The Lord had changed them all in a remarkable way. Their outlook on life and their lifestyle, both emotionally and spiritually, is greatly improved from what I remembered. These Christian individuals shared with me how God had brought about such a noticeable transformation.

The testimony of these changed believers has given me a new challenge to pray for others regarding matters of the emotions and spirit. I never have had particular difficulty in believing that God answers prayer for physical and financial healing and from heinous sins because I've seen many answers to prayer in that line. But these individuals helped me see that God also frees His children from emotional bondage. All four have been freed to serve the Lord with joy and liberty rather than being held captive to themselves and Satan as previously. The truth of Isaiah 49:24-25 is evident in their lives: *"Shall the prey be taken from the mighty, or the lawful captive delivered? But thus saith the Lord, Even the captives of the mighty shall be taken away, and the prey of the terrible shall be delivered; for I will contend with him that contendeth with thee, and I will save thy children."*

One of the most remarkable changes I witnessed was in the life of a woman I had known for years. We were intimate friends of her family. From the time she was a teenager, jealousy and resentment of a family member whom she could not accept or forgive spoiled her relationship with her family and friends. Thoughts of this person and the injustice she felt had been done to her consumed her, making it impossible for her to enjoy any other relationship. She turned away from people who were willing to befriend her and ignored their overtures of friendship. She preferred to be alone to suffer with her own hard feelings. At times, her spirits lifted, but as soon as that family member became the topic of conversation, she plunged back down again.

Finally, through the book of Ephesians, the Holy Spirit revealed to her that her struggle was not with the person, but with the evil spirit behind what had been said and done. She fully recognized the evil powers that influenced her thoughts and attitude, keeping her bound to bitterness and resentment. When she grasped the truth that God was powerful enough to deal with all the injustice (whether real or imaginary), she was able to choose to let the hard feelings go. She became willing to allow God to make things right on her behalf. She agreed to wait in patience for God to bring about a reconciliation, which freed her from the bondage that had enslaved her.

With the harmful feelings melted away, the change in her lifestyle is astonishing! She is now a consistently happy, outgoing receptionist for her husband's profession. She is a good wife and mother. I watched her busily serving others in the local church, smiling the whole time. It was hard to imagine her as the same girl who had been unable to get out of bed in the morning and face life.

Another Christian suffered in much the same way and was unable to stay employed nor take responsibility for his life. He also found it very difficult to talk to people. I was amazed to learn that he is presently working in a company and was influential in getting another brother hired, a man whom he mentors in business and in spiritual things. I could hardly believe my ears when I heard him speak from the platform, adeptly using a large chart to help illustrate his message.

A second brother, who I remembered as too occupied with himself to take life seriously enough to include a wife, is now the head of a lovely family. I was fascinated by the testimony of his dear wife, whom he had married when she was an unsaved person. Following her salvation, this couple chose to serve the Lord by using their home for Him.

I had an enjoyable evening of fellowship with a third brother who spent many hours in our home. I was often surprised by how much of Gifford's time he consumed, while giving nothing in return, or showing any interest in changing. Year after year we saw no visible improvement. But now the sparkle in his eyes proves that he actually enjoys giving much of his time to others, especially to his family members.

These evidences of the power of God started me on a search for the reasons for the amazing changes. I wanted to know why this same deliverance wasn't taking place in the lives of many others who suffered in similar ways. As I prepared a message for a ladies' meeting, John 10:10 came as a possible answer: *"The thief cometh not but for to steal, and to kill, and destroy; I am come that they might have life, and that they might have it more abundantly."*

It is no coincidence that Christ joined the two thoughts of His offer of abundant life and the thief's desire to snatch it away together in one verse. I wondered if the changed people I'd noticed were actually experiencing the abundant life Christ said He came to give. Were their changed facial expressions an evidence of this truth? The more I thought about it, the more convinced I became that the abundant life Christ came to offer comprises joy, peace, and love rather than the material things that we often equate with His blessing.

Although the stories my friends told were vastly different, a common denominator ran through all of them. They told of painful crises that brought them to the point of desperation and caused them to seek Christ more diligently. They had to find Christ as a reality. They all shared the longing Paul expressed in Philippians 3:10: *"That I may know Him, and the power of His resurrection."*

By seeking Christ, they became more aware of the particular sins Satan used to control them—fear, unforgiveness, and worry were the three most common offenders. As they identified their sins, they confessed them, which is all Christ requires of us: *"Having therefore, these promises, dearly beloved, let us cleanse ourselves from all filthiness of the flesh and spirit, perfecting holiness in the fear of God"* (2 Cor. 7:1).

With that, they were able to enter into the abundant life Christ offers. That life is available to all, but there is an enemy who constantly tries to steal, kill, and destroy it. After a Christian has received the life Christ offers, Satan can't touch the soul. However, he often succeeds in stealing the truth, killing the believer's joy, and destroying the believer's testimony. Only by constant confession of sin can he be kept out.

The vigilance on my behalf of two very dear friends illustrates this for me. As soon as these friends heard that my daughter had moved out and was living separately, they became concerned for my safety. They took it upon themselves to secure my home by installing extra locks. They made sure that no thief would enter to steal my possessions in my absence or threaten my life when I was at home alone. As a result of their concern and generosity I have a feeling of security whether I am at home or not. Every night I make a circuit of the house, making sure the locks are all in use.

There is a link between my new locks and keeping watch on our minds. These changed individuals I have mentioned became aware that they needed to check the locks on their minds, confessing their sins lest Satan should sneak in to steal, kill, and destroy the abundant life Christ came to give them. By choice, they put on the armor of God to protect themselves. By deliberately putting on Christ as truth, Christ as righteousness, Christ as shield, and Christ as the Living Word, they were freed from their prisons of self. It is simple to put these truths into the life. Yet it is so easy to neglect or forget to practice these basics. Christ came to give abundant life to whoever chooses to receive it. It is as much ours for the taking as our salvation.

19
VEXATION OR VICTORY?

A conversation with an evangelist prompted my thinking on the difference between living in vexation or victory. He was going through a time of testing and was down spiritually to the point at which he was ready to throw in the towel, call it quits, and get back to the "real world." He had had enough! Like David, his feet had very nearly slipped. As we talked together, I detected that he was comparing his life to that of the people around him. He was wondering if giving up a lucrative position had been worth the sacrifice. He was not comparing his life to that of the unsaved, rather he was comparing it to that of Christians who lived year after year enjoying a comfortable living, even self-indulgence, while his family struggled to get along on a minimal income.

As we talked, my friend attempted to sort out a few things, and I was his sounding board. Finally, he came to the point of agreeing with David: *"When I thought to know this, it was too painful for me, until I went into the sanctuary of God, then understood I their end"* (Ps. 73:16-17).

When I think back to the conversation, Hebrews 4:12-13 comes to mind:

For the Word of God is quick and powerful, and sharper than any two-edged sword, piercing even to the dividing asunder of soul and spirit, and of the joints and marrow, and is a discerner of the thoughts and intents of the heart. Neither is there any creature that is not manifest in His sight, but all things are naked and opened unto the eyes of Him with whom we have to do.

I find that comparing scripture with scripture is profitable because the Word of God is its own best commentary. Situations written about in the Old Testament are mentioned again in the New Testament. By reading and meditating on the Word of God we gain insight, understand mysteries, and obtain answers to many of life's puzzles when we link the original story with comments made later in the Bible. Second Peter 2:7-8 is one such example. Hebrews 11 is another portion of Scripture where the author puts the names of some people in the "Hall of Faith," yet when we read about them in the Old Testament, their lives were anything but perfect.

Peter, for example, declares Lot to be a just and righteous man, then adds that he was a vexed man the whole time he seemed to be living on easy street in Sodom. Lot accumulated wealth, prestige, and popularity while living in Sodom, however it amounted to vanity and vexation and he did not experience the peace of God in his inner self. Although Lot clearly believed in God, a knowledge he gained while living with his aunt Sarah and uncle Abraham, he made some unhappy choices. The results were vexation and frustration.

The salvation of the servants of the Lord is not dependent on their good works any more than anyone is saved by works. Our eternal rewards and our present peace, however, are very much determined by what we do in this life. Scripture reminds us, as in the case of Lot, *"If any man's work shall be burned, he shall suffer loss: but he himself shall be saved; yet so as by fire"* (1 Cor. 3:15).

My evangelist friend was not slipping into a life of sin; he was just discouraged and wanted to give up his service for the Lord. Lest you wonder what happened to him, I assure you he chose to continue trusting the Lord, and did not stop preaching. Thank God that he remained faithful to the end of his life. His faith energized a renewed interest in His service to the Lord. He realized that he could lose his crown and forfeit his eternal rewards if he quit early. The loss of a victorious, happy life on earth would have carried over into eternity.

Thinking of lost rewards brings to mind an experience I had on Mother's Day when I was eleven years old. In the days before school buses, children from rural areas sometimes had to move into town in order to attend school. Our home was always open to the children from believing farm families who wanted to attend school. The girls who lived with us at the time had talked among themselves about gifts for my mother, but I had completely forgotten to buy or make a gift for her. The day arrived, and I was not prepared. As I saw the gifts given to my mother, I felt terrible. I was one miserable girl. Even though Mother assured me that she understood, I cried the rest of the day until I couldn't cry anymore. I just could not believe that I had been so thoughtless and negligent. It was devastating to know I had done so poorly for my mother.

When my evangelist friend asked if I found working for crowns to be enough incentive to work for the Lord, I immediately remembered my feelings as I watched the girls give presents to Mom as I stood by empty-handed. Simultaneously, Revelation 4:10 came to mind: "The four and twenty elders...cast their crowns before the throne, saying, 'Thou art worthy, O Lord, to receive glory and honor and power: for Thou hast created all things, and for Thy pleasure they are and were created.'"

Earning eternal rewards is not a matter of pridefully walking around heaven with jewels glittering in our crowns. Rather, it is a matter of having something to give back to our Lord in love and respect. I would not want to stand before Christ at His judgment seat and be as miserable as I was on that particular Mother's Day. If I didn't receive some reward, then I would be empty-handed there also. I highly doubt that I would be any less regretful than I was on that unforgettable Mother's Day. I want very much to have something to give to Him on that day, but we must first receive our crowns before we have anything to lay at His feet. Rewards, you see, are for the eternal glory of the Giver, not the recipient. That He was able to accomplish anything at all with us will be cause for our wonder and our worship.

If you have realized that you are living a life of a vexed Lot, God knows how to deliver you, but you must choose to let Him. You can exchange a life of vexation for a life of victory. Matthew 20:1-16 has often been a great comfort because it reminds me that it is never too late, as long as we live, to accept God's invitation to work in His vineyard. Our Master is righteous. He will give us our rightful pay for our work. There are always things we can do for Him regardless of our age. May God grant us the joy of Proverbs 4:18-19: *"But the path of the just is as the shining light, that shineth more and more unto the perfect day. The way of the wicked is as darkness; they know not at what they stumble."*

20
JOCHEBED

A verse popped into my head and I can't keep it out of my mind. I believe the Lord wants me to put it down on paper: *"And Pharaoh's daughter said unto her [Jochebed], 'Take this child away, and nurse it for me, and I will give thee thy wages.' The woman took the child and nursed it"* (Ex. 2:9).

Jochebed took that darling baby Moses out of the princess' arms and oh-so-thankfully took him home to nurse him. Can you imagine her thoughts as she carried him home? It must have been a great effort on her part not to let her joy show too much. She would not want the princess to surmise that she was the mother and change her mind about letting her take the baby. Although I'm sure Jochebed would have gladly paid the princess for the privilege of caring for her own baby, the princess promised wages for her efforts.

Jochebed considered this opportunity to be given directly from the Lord God of Israel. I believe Jochebed knew that Moses was a special child who would be used by God (Heb. 11:23). The same faith she had exhibited in hiding him also gave her courage to train him and entrust him to the Lord. While she nursed Moses physically, she also trained him emotionally and spiritually for the Lord. She taught him from an early age about the Living God. Moses saw the faith of his mother and it greatly influenced his life. We have proof of his faith in the following years.

Jochebed was a very special mother because she trained three leaders of Israel (Mic. 6:4). Moses' older brother Aaron and his sister Miriam were also in places of responsibility. This speaks well for her, doesn't it?

Moses was brought up in a slave's home but was taught to look beyond circumstances to eternity. He saw the suffering of God's people by living with his parents who were treated like slaves. No doubt he was told the story of how his parents had risked their lives to hide him from the king's soldiers. Later, his life in the palace offered all the pleasures of affluence, yet he chose his former life with its lack of comfort and pleasures (Heb. 11:23-29). He must have been criticized for leaving the palace and the woman who had saved his life. Some probably considered him to be ungrateful for his care and education.

Yet God wanted Moses for His very own. In living out his commitment to God, he chose to live separately from the world around him. He honored God and saw the world through the eyes of faith. Jochebed's godly influence had taught Moses to esteem *"the reproach of Christ greater riches than the treasure in Egypt; for he had respect unto the recompense of the reward"* (Heb. 11:26).

When Moses heard the word "Messiah," he doubtless remembered what his mother had taught him about the promised One who would come to deliver the Israelites from their sins. Moses had heard the Scriptures enough to know who the Messiah was. He believed the promises God had made to His people. He had a special insight into God's purposes for His people and believed they were to be separated from the world around them.

Let me encourage every young mother to take her children as from the Lord and to raise them for Him. Children who are raised for the Lord are equipped to make the same choices Moses did and enjoy the same results that Moses is enjoying to this day. This encouragement is not limited to mothers only; it includes every woman who is a nurse, a camp counselor, a school or Sunday school teacher, or a single sister whose life touches the life of a child.

Your wages for your service will be saved up for you in the

bank of heaven. Even if the results are not the same as Jochebed's, you will be rewarded well by God for your work. Because of the child's free will, not all properly raised children will become obedient like Moses. But God's wages are for the labor, not for the child's accomplishments.

It is important to remember that in this life credit is not always given where credit is due. Not too many people today remember Jochebed's name. However, think of the abundant rejoicing upon her entrance into heaven! We want the children who are entrusted to our care to have the spiritual resources to make the same wise, eternal choices as Moses did when they reach adulthood.

We pray that our potential spiritual leaders will be willing to seek the eternal riches of Christ rather than the treasures of this world. By learning to build their lives on the Rock—Christ Jesus—they will be able to stand firm in the face of adversity when the sea is in front of them and the enemy's army is drawing closer by the minute. It is only when we, as Christian women, have confidence in and an appreciation of Christ that we can instill the same in the children whose lives we touch.

21
A BASIC LESSON

It was an embarrassing and frustrating evening. I had left the weekly meeting at our local church early because I was out of sorts with my husband. I was depressed and angry. The old, nagging feeling that Gifford had taken advantage of me, combined with an inner struggle for my own identity, was making me miserable. As I backed the car out of the parking lot, it accidentally slipped into a nearby irrigation ditch, which only magnified my troubles.

No matter how hard I tried, I couldn't get the car to budge. Neighbors, who saw my predicament, came to help me but in spite of the many hands and a multitude of suggestions, the car would not be pushed or pulled out. By that time, the service was over. In desperation I went back into the building to find my husband. Due to the tension that had been building up in me and between us for some time, it was a difficult decision. I very much wanted to prove to Gifford that I could do it myself.

The independent spirit, with which I had trouble before we married, had surfaced again. Soon after our engagement, Gifford had changed churches, causing an uneasy feeling about the woman's role in the church and home. I began to have doubts about our upcoming marriage and gave him his ring back. However, weeks passed without any peace of mind, and by the time he called to ask if he could come for a visit, I was more than ready to invite him over again. It only took a short walk to convince me that I was in love and wanted to be a part of his life. God would help us work out our differences.

107

We both felt that God had chosen us as a team to serve Him on the mission field, and the Lord blessed our commitment. However, recently I had permitted a gradual unrest to sneak in and spoil things. It came to a climax that night.

I left Gifford to figure out how to rescue the stranded car and walked home. With each step I grew more upset as I tried to justify my position. Once home, I quickly washed up and got ready for bed. I felt duty-bound to have my devotions, but I cut them short and turned in early. Needless to say, sleep would not come.

Although this is recorded on paper in a matter of minutes, in reality it took a couple of hours for Gifford to get the car out of the ditch. While he was working on the car, I was working through my feelings. I tossed and turned, trying to straighten out my thoughts. The Lord brought 1 Peter 2:23b before me and convinced me that, even if Gifford was wrong in what he was doing, God could intervene on my behalf. When I came to the point at which I could allow God to handle what seemed to me to be an injustice and turn it all into a blessing, various other portions of Scripture came to mind. Through those Scriptures, I was convicted of my wrong attitude toward Gifford and even worse, my wrong attitude toward the Lord. I saw that when I was rebelling against my circumstances and God's order for the home, I was actually rebelling against His sovereignty! I had forgotten the goodness and patience of God. With the awareness of each sin, I confessed it to the Lord. The peace that flooded my heart defies description.

A new confidence in the Lord's ability to work all things out for my good calmed my spirit. I decided that God truly was good and that I could completely trust Him, as Judge of all the earth, to do righteously. God brought to mind that Gifford was a good man and sought first to please Him. I began to see how fortunate I was to be married to a man of Gifford's spiritual caliber. Many other things for which I should have been thankful flashed before me. I knew then that I was ready to whole-heartedly apologize to my husband and start over with God's help.

I see now more than ever that commitment brings freedom and joy. Christ was our greatest Example. He committed Himself to His Father who judges all things righteously. Isaiah reminds us that Christ was not rebellious, nor could He sin. As a human, He did not easily welcome suffering, but His relationship with the Father was such that He trusted Him implicitly. That trust enabled Him to willingly sacrifice Himself.

Within minutes of my decision, I heard Gifford drive in. He was soon leaping up the stairs two at a time as he always did when in a good mood. He walked into our bedroom with his usual big smile, clapped his hands together and said something to the effect that the car was home again. He seemed completely oblivious to my anger, which by now was completely gone. Instead of blowing up at him as I would have wanted to earlier, I smiled back and jumped to my feet. With not just a few tears, I made the apologies that I had promised the Lord I would make. When Gifford took me in his arms, I knew that he had completely forgiven me.

I only wish that I could end this story with the words "and they lived happily ever after." That would not be entirely true, but that night certainly marked a turning point in our marriage. With a common love for the Lord and much prayer, we gradually ironed out our differences. Our love and understanding for each other deepened.

My doctrine shall drop as the rain, my speech shall distill as the dew, as the small rain upon the tender herb, and as the showers upon the grass: because I will proclaim the Name of the Lord; ascribe ye greatness unto our God. He is the Rock, His work is perfect; for all His ways are judgment; a God of truth and without iniquity, just and right is He (Deut. 32:2-4).

22
IT IS I, BE NOT AFRAID

One thing that makes decisions so hard to make is the variety of advice given by well-meaning friends. Some of it you may ask for, but most of it comes voluntarily. The moment the doctor told my husband that his illness was terminal, he planned to go back to Japan. He wanted to be buried there and had plenty he wanted to do before his death. Many people felt this was not advisable and tried to discourage us from going.

Uncertain of what to do, I had a consultation with Gifford's doctor and asked him if he thought I was foolish to agree with Gifford and take such a sick man on such a long trip. Without any hesitation, he said, "Go for it! If he wants to go back so badly, why not let him have his last wish? But do it soon." He then provided detailed written instructions as to what to do in case Gifford needed medical attention on the way.

After prayerfully weighing the pros and cons, I agreed to go. We began preparations immediately, crossing the United States by car in short, easy stages. I was worried about the long journey across the ocean and wondered how well he would tolerate the long plane trip. He was always airsick, even under normal conditions.

As we boarded the plane, I realized that the Lord had already gone before us and arranged for the right flight attendant to be on duty. The dear woman took one glance at Gifford and told us not to get too settled in our front-row seats. Soon she returned and invited him to follow her. She had cleared the seats of the back row of the plane by asking folks to fill in the empty seats here and there. She brought pillows and blankets and settled him in more comfortably than any nurse could have done. With the help of a sleeping pill, he slept nearly the whole way over.

Gifford was so grateful to be back in Japan. God had granted him his wish, and I have never regretted following through with his plans. It is clear to me that Gifford's desires were given to him by Christ, who later gave the strength needed for every situation as it arose. He used countless numbers of His people to accomplish this.

We spent two or three days in Tokyo with missionary friends before tackling the final lap of our journey home to Takasaki. Our friends put on a new tape they had just received, and one of the first songs was "The King Is Coming." It was the first time either one of us had heard the song, and I can still feel the tingle start up my spine as I picture the scene—the procession of marching bands, people thronging the streets, and the chariot carrying the Messiah in all of His glory with the banner "King of Kings" preceding Him. As we listened, all the stress that had built up during the long trip from Chicago to Tokyo was released. Our tears flowed at the thought of our Lord's future glory. Some day it would be worth it all! Our friends kindly left the room as Gifford and I held each other. A renewed hope of eternal life together after our King returns and takes us to His eternal home filled our hearts. Not only was our weariness erased, we had fresh strength to return to our home, settle in, and make plans for the remaining months of his life. For the time being, at least, fear of the future was gone.

It would be wonderful if this type of experience could be permanent, but in my case it has not been that way. I awoke from sleep one night after having a nightmarish dream of being separated from my beloved. I couldn't shake the dream. It only added to the darkness I felt because of what might lie ahead for us. Then, the story of the famous boat ride the disciples took on the Sea of Galilee suddenly came to mind. I realized that the disciples were exactly where they found themselves because Christ had commanded them to be there. So were we! In the darkness, the words, *"It is I, be not afraid"* popped into my head. Nothing about my circumstances changed, but I felt the balm of Gilead pour over me. The peace that only the Lord gives came with those six words, *"It is I, be not afraid."* Christ was saying to me, "I'm out here; trust Me." Although I'd heard those words many times before, I had never heard them with the force of meaning and the calming effect they had on me then. With a new attitude towards Gifford's illness, I turned over and went back to sleep.

On another occasion, the Lord confirmed His presence with an equally strong sense of His peace. Gifford was in the hospital in Tokyo, recuperating from another one of his major surgeries. I was returning from a visit with him and had just had a consultation with his doctor—neither of which had been the least bit encouraging. The subway train on which I was riding became an elevated train for a short time before it plunged underground again. I looked out and thought how Tokyo, with its neon signs in different colors, looked like a huge Christmas tree. One short sign caught my eye. It consisted of only three letters and made no sense at all. I moved my head to see if part of the sign was hidden, but it wasn't. The sign was high in the air and read "CAN"—that was all.

I was puzzled by what the sign could be advertising, but the private message the sign conveyed to me was clear: "I CAN, I can be as much comfort and strength to you as Gifford ever was." At first, I resisted the message. I wanted Gifford to live and continue to be that for me. Gradually, I accepted the fact of what the doctor had told me. I put that truth together with the truth Christ had promised: *"I can do all things through Christ which strengtheneth me"* (Phil. 4:13). That message touched my heart. Christ breathed that message into my soul many times during the months that followed.

On successive trips past that same area, I looked for the

sign. I did not find the "CAN" until I saw the whole sign lit up: "CANADA DRY." Imagine finding ginger ale in Tokyo! But that sign had advertised to me a far more refreshing drink than ginger ale ever could be, and I'm still going on the refreshment that it offered.

As I write this, I have experienced twenty-four years of widowhood. So to you who may be facing widowhood or the loneliness of singleness, let me say we CAN do all things through Christ who strengthens us. We CAN do whatever He has planned for us, although it may not be what we have in mind for ourselves. If Christ can do it through me, He can do it through you, too.

Let's be careful to give credit where credit is due—to Christ Jesus our Lord. The world says, "Pull yourself together, find other interests, and get busy." I have been given plenty of similar messages, but I haven't had the power to put them into permanent use without Christ. When He sees me rowing extra hard, just as the disciples did to keep afloat, He draws alongside of me and offers the same words, *"It is I, be not afraid. I will do it."*

23
A JEALOUS GOD

Last night I heard an unusual story that caused me to awaken this morning thinking about God's reason for saying He is a jealous God. A visitor told me of a friend who had confided that although she was engaged to one young man, she was still writing to a couple of other men in an intimate way. My visitor had trusted and admired this woman, but after learning of this, she lost respect for her. I did too. I wanted to immediately advise her fiancé of the situation and urge him to break their engagement until she could completely and unreservedly give him her whole heart.

This situation is unthinkable. I cringe at the thought of such a marriage. The woman is still clinging to other men as possibilities in case something goes wrong between her and her fiancé. How I want to spare this young man the misery that is sure to follow if his wife-to-be can't completely entrust herself to him.

Unless the woman gets this fundamental issue right, it's unlikely that she will be able to enjoy the bliss God intends for marriage. Even if she hasn't been guilty of physical involvement with these other men, how can she ever be "one" with a man to whom she has been unfaithful in her mind? As memories of past relationships crowd in, intimacy of their marriage will be spoiled. Her fiancé has a reason, and a right, to be jealous of other suitors as long as she is engaged to him.

In the Old Testament, God often charged His people with the same offense. He accused them of saying they loved Him while they toyed with friendships that were not acceptable and trusted other sources for their happiness. James 4:4 is a New Testament expression of the same accusation: *"Ye adulterers and adulteresses, know ye not that the friendship of the world is enmity with God? Whosoever, therefore will be a friend of the world is the enemy of God."*

Most of us would agree that infidelity is unacceptable in the marriage relationship. But we generally find it more difficult to recognize infidelity in our relationship with God. When I'm under stress, for example, I often find myself seeking support and answers from my human relationships rather than trusting God to meet my needs. I unconsciously reason that if the Lord doesn't wish to answer my prayers in the way I imagine He should, or doesn't come through to my liking, I then have someone or something—money, friends, family, and so forth—to fall back on.

God admits that He is jealous when I do this because He reads my thoughts and knows my double-mindedness—in the same way that the man mentioned above has a right to be angry about the woman's other lovers, God has a right to be jealous of my involvements with other people, things, or activities that I believe will meet my needs when it appears that He will not meet them. In 1 John 2:15-17, John puts it this way:

> *Love not the world, neither the things that are in the world. If any [wo]man love the world, the love of the Father is not in him. For all that is in the world, the lust of the flesh, and the lust of the eyes, and the pride of life, is not of the Father, but is of the world. And the world passeth away, and the lust thereof; but [s]he that doeth the will of God abideth forever.*

The story of the engaged young woman conveyed a very personal message to me from the Lord. He was asking me to make a fresh commitment to Him as my prospective Bridegroom. I was just as guilty of flirting with the things of this life as the young woman being unfaithful to her fiancé.

The Lord has often used the tiny book of Ruth, tucked away

in the Old Testament, to encourage me in the past. As I thought about this topic, God used it once again to challenge me by bringing Boaz to mind. Before, when reading the book of Ruth, I was mostly taken up with Ruth's faithfulness and love of her mother-in-law. But as I reread this story, I saw afresh the love and graciousness of Boaz.

Although he was a mighty and wealthy man, Boaz had a tender heart. He was aware of Ruth and constantly watched out for her welfare. He invited her to eat with his workers. He thought of the smallest details to make her life more comfortable. Boaz certainly would have been justified in being jealous if Ruth had started sending letters back to her childhood sweethearts in Moab in order to nurture other relationships just in case Boaz didn't measure up to her expectations.

I recognize many of Boaz's characteristics in my prospective Bridegroom, the Lord Jesus Christ. He is constantly aware of my needs and provides for my comfort, just as Boaz did for Ruth. I recall how, in 1975, the Lord used the book of Ruth to guide me in making a fresh commitment to Him when I returned to Japan following Gifford's death. I had begun to question why I had gone back to Japan. I felt very aware of the fact that I wasn't as skillful in Japanese, nor could I teach as well as Gifford. Because I didn't have the energy or zeal he had, I was comparing myself to him all the time and felt more miserable by the minute. I was feeling very inadequate to be able to do missionary work alone.

But one day while I was reading Ruth, my eyes became glued to verse 8 of chapter 2: *"Neither go from hence, but abide here fast by my maidens."*

It was as if God spoke to me from heaven. He reminded me that He would provide everything I needed for gleaning in His field. I might not be as gifted a worker as Gifford was, but I could be one who gleans. I could still pray and encourage believers.

Suddenly I realized I'd been so occupied comparing myself

117

to my late husband, that I'd practically forgotten the dozens of single women who needed a sympathetic, listening ear, who needed friendship, who needed encouragement in dealing with their special problems. As I read on, verse 21 caught my attention: *"He said unto me also, thou shalt keep fast by my young men, until they have ended all my harvest."*

The Lord then brought to my mind the men, still young in years, who had stepped in to take over the many phases of work Gifford had left behind. There were two assemblies and another in the making that were being shepherded by men who had little experience, although they were faithful men who had leadership potential. There was also a bookstore and a camp for which others had assumed responsibility. I wanted to help and encourage the young Christian men and their wives who were passing through their spiritual adolescence. There were many pitfalls ahead for all of them. It would take time before they were established in the Lord's service. I then became confident that God wanted me to stay in Japan to glean behind these reapers. Through the power of His Word, I could, and did, face life with a definite purpose.

To this day, I have never regretted that decision. Christ has given me the love, care, and protection that far surpasses that of Boaz for Ruth. As I read the story today and reflected on the special lunches, the handfuls of grain left on purpose, and the bonus ephahs of barley, my love for my waiting Bridegroom was rekindled. I want my heart to be hungry only for Him. I can hardly wait for the marriage that awaits me. I don't want to give my prospective Bridegroom any reason to be jealous.

24
BY MY SPIRIT

The three-story building stood as a witness to the Lord's goodness. It looked more like a miracle to me. It truly was not built by might nor by human power, but totally by the Lord. It was God's provision from beginning to end, both physically and financially.

Physically, Gifford had returned to Japan for the purpose of building this store, even though he was in the last stages of cancer. God spared his life until the building was finished and his work as overseer was complete. From his bedroom window, Gifford watched the furnishings being moved in. We carried him into the building to see the finished work. He died less than ten days after seeing his twenty-year-old dream for a Christian bookstore in the area become a reality.

Financially, the building was built at a time when medical bills for Gifford's care were the highest. Yet everything was on schedule, and the bills were paid on time. The Hikari Shoten (Light Bookstore) was built and stocked totally free of debt.

The opening day was a huge success. People came from far and wide to celebrate. The Lord had proven once more to us Ephesians 3:20: *"Now unto Him who is able to do exceeding abundantly above all that we ask or think, according to the power that worketh in us. Unto Him be glory..."*

The Lord supplied just the right couple to manage the store, and they moved into the apartment provided for the manager in the same building. I was as happy as Gifford was to see it all happen just as he had planned, prayed, and worked for so many years. His joy was contagious, and it cushioned the pain of seeing him fail daily.

A couple of years after Gifford had gone home to be with the Lord, however, the bottom suddenly fell out of everything. My bubble burst. The father of the manager's wife had a massive stroke, so they suddenly had to move to another city to help care for him. Our well-thought-out plans abruptly ended at this turn of events. I knew my limitations. I also knew that a Christian bookstore in Buddhist Japan would not take in enough revenue to hire a full-time clerk until it was more well-known. I was devastated, discouraged, and overwhelmed by the responsibility. I had no idea which way to turn.

Part-time help was hired, but I knew it would not work over the long run. Nevertheless, God had a plan. It was one I would never have thought of myself.

The young mothers of the assembly took on the bookstore needs as a special prayer project. As they prayed, they thought of a plan to work together to keep the store open. They worked out a rotating schedule whereby one of them was always at the store to answer the phone and sell literature every afternoon. They did a super job and made friends of every customer. A school teacher in the assembly felt the burden to accept the responsibility as manager, and his wife did the bookkeeping. He read everything that was sold in the store to ensure nothing would ever hinder anyone's faith in Christ or cause doubts and confusion. I stood by and saw God bring it all together.

I fully expected the enthusiasm to wane. I thought the burden would grow heavier month after month as each busy mother took her turn in the store. Instead, it had the opposite effect. The believers were drawn closer through their planning, working, and praying together. They began to feel that it was their store. They had a great interest in keeping the display window attractive and inviting. Volunteer help kept the store open and operating in the black until it was well established and drawing customers from the surrounding cities.

Even the presence of young children in the store did not hinder the ministry. As a whole, the Japanese are a patient, courteous people. The toddlers only added to the friendly atmosphere. The ladies' group bought a playpen (which was a new thing in Japan) so babies could be kept off the floor and out of the hands of every well-meaning customer who came into the store. Customers enjoyed reading books to the children, while learning a lot too!

In the meantime, the Lord prepared an excellent single woman as a salesclerk. She and her mother moved into the apartment above the store and she worked as the salesclerk for many years, while she took care of her elderly mother. As I reviewed God's detailed provision, I thought of Zechariah 4:6: *"Not by might, nor by power, but by My Spirit, saith the Lord of hosts."*

It truly was the Spirit of God who enabled these women to care for their homes, their children, and to keep the customers happy, too. Comfortable chairs formed a circle in one corner where interested people could hear the gospel. There, too, believers were encouraged and strengthened in the Lord. Many lasting friendships were formed over a cup of tea and "sembei" (rice crackers). The store became a meeting place for the saved and unbelievers alike. Once again, the Lord turned what seemed like an utterly impossible situation into a tremendous blessing. Twenty-five years later, it still has a wide testimony, great influence, and is being used by the Lord in an effective way.

25
THE SYROPHOENICIAN WOMAN

Sometimes when reading the Bible, I have a strong desire to pattern my life after the person about whom I am reading. This dear woman living north of Canaan in Phoenicia (modern Lebanon) is a good example (Mt. 15:21-28). Her story challenges me in the matter of acceptance and persistence every time I read it.

The woman cried out to Christ, begging Him to heal her demon-possessed daughter. She pleaded with Him to have mercy on her. He remained silent and didn't answer her right away, yet she did not stop calling out to Him. His disciples told Him to send her away because she was a nuisance. Still she didn't give up. Finally, He spoke to her but not to grant her request. Instead, He reminded her that she wasn't deserving of His help and inferred that she had been born into the wrong race. I admire her humble and submissive response. I am amazed by the way she did not resist, rebel, or question His response. Rather, she stayed until she received her request.

Instead of questioning Christ as to why she was not born an Israelite, or arguing, or trying to manipulate Him, or claiming that life was unfair, she listened to what He said and agreed. But she did not end it there. She drew closer to worship Him. She reminded Him that even the dogs get the crumbs that fall from the master's table and patiently waited for Him to hear her plea and heal her daughter. Claiming no right to sit at His table, she did not accuse God of giving her a disturbed child. Nor did she express any self-justification or dissatisfaction.

How, I wonder, was she able to accept her lot in life so

meekly? It is one thing to wait and quite another to wait as patiently as she did. In Psalm 40:1-6, David bears testimony to what he received from the Lord—because he, too, waited patiently. He lists the benefits he received from waiting in faith and placing his hope in God: God heard him, brought him out of a pit (sin? depression? doubts?), set his feet upon the solid Rock and established him, and gave him a brand new song of praise to the Lord. Have you felt you needed God to help you change your tune? David received everything he needed. Many readers through the ages have been influenced by reading his words. Perhaps this dear sister was one of them.

I woke in the middle of the night with a knuckle that hurt so badly I couldn't get back to sleep. The pain was not bone or muscle pain, it was in the skin. Rather than lie in bed and worry about an infection, I got up to examine it under a bright light. Equipping myself with a magnifying glass, needle, and some hydrogen peroxide, I started to probe. After seeing the peroxide fizz up in earnest, I knew I had an infection deep down that I had merely covered with a band-aid. After a few jabs, I saw a tiny dark speck, and when I probed a bit further, a huge sliver popped out. How a sliver that size could have gotten under my skin without my being aware of it was a puzzle to me. Within seconds after the object was out and the surrounding area was cleaned up, the pain completely stopped. It's hard for me to believe I put up with the pain without trying to find its source. I couldn't see the sliver so I didn't think it was there. The simple tools I used did the job and brought relief. I woke in the morning with a normal finger.

As unlikely as it may seem, I see a link between my experience with the sliver in my hand, David being rewarded for patiently waiting for God to grant his requests, and the story of the dear Syrophoenician woman. Christ commended her for her faith and praised her for it. Our faith is tested and strengthened when God requires us to wait. Her story has encouraged me to be more accepting, persistent, and patient when making requests to God. At the same time, I need to find the slivers that cause so much pain and hinder God from working in my life.

Because of unbelief and impatience when God is not granting my requests immediately, I get discouraged far too easily. Yet if Christ really is Lord and reigns supreme in my life, then why the self-pity when God is silent for a time and wants me to wait? If He is Lord, doesn't He have the right to ask me to wait—or even say "no"? Why the resistance to what He is permitting to happen in my life or the needless worry and fretting? It is one thing to sing "Our God Reigns" on Sunday morning, but quite another to believe that He is in complete control and go back to sleep in the middle of the night in peace, assurance, and faith.

I also realize that issues as insignificant as slivers are often my resistance toward the circumstances I am facing at the time. How much more profitable it would be to reach for the needle and remove these specks instead of using a band-aid to cover up the problem. Tiny specks fester and cause real trouble when they aren't removed immediately. I'll admit that it is more painful to remove the specks, but fewer infections result.

Non-acceptance and impatience may seem to be small specks, but they can cause much pain if we do not deal with them. We need to look for the specks that are causing infection in our lives and clean them up so we can receive healing from God. In time, if we wait patiently in faith for God to grant us our requests, we will receive many benefits, as David did. Like the Syrophoenician woman, we must keep on persistently asking and not allow ourselves to become discouraged.

26
MICAH'S MOM

The seventeenth chapter of Judges is one of the most frightening and challenging chapters in the Bible: *"And there was a
man of mount Ephraim, whose name was Micah. And he said unto
his mother, The eleven hundred shekels of silver that were taken from
thee, about which thou cursedst, and spakest of also in mine ears,
behold, the silver is with me; I took it. And his mother said, Blessed
be thou of the Lord, my son"* (Jud. 17:1-2).

It was especially thought-provoking, as I read further, to
discover the consequences of both Micah's and his mother's
actions. She was as guilty as he was in introducing idols into
their home, their extended family, and later into the whole
nation of Israel. One day she and her son will stand before
God to give an account of their actions.

Micah had stolen money from her, and when he returned it,
she did not reprimand him. Instead of making him aware of
his sin, she blessed him! Micah's mother was so relieved her
stolen money was accounted for, that she missed an opportunity to impress on her son the seriousness of stealing. Getting
her money back meant more to her than her son's righteousness. She treated the situation as if he had sinned only against
her. The punishment of the whole nation of Israel through cap-
tivity might have been avoided had she exhorted him to go to
the tabernacle with a sacrifice for sin. Instead of encouraging
him to ask for God's mercy, and to receive His forgiveness, she
excused him. She overlooked his sin because she didn't think
he had done anything all that bad.

Their breach of God's law soon led to an even greater sin in

God's sight. The mother took shekels of the money and gave them to a silversmith to have him make idols. She then brought them home and set them up in Micah's house:

> When he had restored the eleven hundred shekels of silver to his mother, his mother said, I had wholly dedicated the silver unto the Lord from my hand for my son, to make a graven image and a molten image: now therefore I will restore it unto thee. Yet he restored the money unto his mother; and his mother took two hundred shekels of silver, and gave them to the founder, who made thereof a graven image and a molten image: and they were in the house of Micah. (Jud. 17:3-4).

Idolatry soon spread through all of Israel.

There was so much spiritual confusion at the time that I doubt she was aware of what she had done. The spiritual state of Israel was such that the people could not differentiate between the instructions of the one, true, living God and the practices assimilated from the heathen nations surrounding them. The biblical concept of priest, ephods, and teraphim were all mixed up with man's ideas of carved images and man-appointed priests. While the people continued with certain rituals God had given them, they also served other gods. Everything was dedicated to the Lord, which supposedly made it all right. However, the result of compromise always brings confusion, which is the beginning of a downward slide.

Zephaniah complained about the same double-mindedness in his generation. Zephaniah 1:5 speaks of: *"them that worship the host of heaven upon the housetops; and them that worship and that swear by the Lord, and that swear by Malcham."*

The people were worshiping and swearing by the creation rather than the Creator.

I wonder if much of the confusion felt in the Christian world today does not stem from the same source. Lack of discernment and obedience always brings confusion and unrest. We don't see many graven images in our Christian world.

However, we have our own forms of idols that spread into the Christian community just as quickly as they did during Micah's time. Paul plainly reminded the saints of Galatia that if they sowed to the flesh (if they sowed the thoughts of the world about them), they would reap of the flesh.

God forbids idolatry and punishes the breaking of the first commandment. We are required to love God with all our hearts. Our worship and devotion belong to God and to God alone. Micah and his mother's actions and their wrong definition of worship replaced the love and adoration God wanted and expected from them.

Sin usually starts simply. Insidiously, it enters our hearts before we know it. Take David's sin with Bathsheba, for instance. It all started in such an innocent way—merely a look. Here again, the responsibility is not all David's. Bathsheba shares equally in their sin. She was not taken by force to the king's quarters. Rather, she went into his room of her own free will. Although she may have risked her life if she had refused him, and had David been that type of king (which I don't think he was), wouldn't death have been a more honorable choice than the heinous sin that led to her husband's death? Think of the misery and shame she would have spared King David, her husband, and herself had she suggested that they bring God into the situation and immediately reminded him that God said, *"Thou shalt not commit adultery."* The tragic results could have been avoided.

In Micah and his mother's choice, it was a case of material idols. In David and Bathsheba's life, it was an idol of a different nature. They chose a few pleasant moments over God's blessing on their lives. Anything can become an idol if we think it will bring us greater happiness than God's blessing. So there is a real danger when Christians take the advice given by various voices in the world around us in preference to the straight-forward commands of the Scriptures. We somehow think God permits us to worship and serve other man-made idols. In truth, God expects total allegiance to Him alone.

We often have an inaccurate definition of God's blessings. His blessings are not the warm, fuzzy feelings we get from Him. God's blessings are really His goodness to us. They are not necessarily to be judged by the effect they have on our happiness. Rather, His goodness produces character, spiritual strength, purity of soul, and loyalty to Christ. God knows the benefits of these attributes and strives in one way or another to produce them in us, to make us like His Son.

Sad to say, we often kick and scream or sulk and pout when we are deprived of our pet desires. We confuse material blessings with spiritual blessings and quickly assume that God has forgotten us. But take a moment to read Paul's list of God's blessing in Ephesians 1:3-8. Not one of them is material!

One short trip back to the Cross will show us how intolerant of sin God has always been. He hated it to the extent that He sent His Son to Calvary in His great display of righteousness. God declared: the soul that sins must die. Therefore, He was duty-bound by His character to keep His Word and sacrifice His Son in order to satisfy His righteousness.

In Micah and his mother's case, we see no evidence of repentance or sacrifice. They influenced the nation of Israel to accept idolatry. In David's life, however, we read of his repentance and God's forgiveness of his sin (Ps. 32 and 51). Such forgiveness, plus the mercy and graciousness of God, brought forth praise and thanksgiving that blesses us even to this day. Surely such goodness deserves our worship!

As Christian men and women, we do well to remember what we do in our homes. The advice we give our children can have as far-reaching an influence—for good or bad—on generations to come as the advice of Micah's mother.

"He that covereth his sins shall not prosper, but whoso confesseth and forsaketh them shall have mercy" (Prov. 28:13).

27
WHAT WENT WRONG?

Miriam was quite a lady. The more I think about her life, the more fascinated I am with her as a person. The story told about her in Exodus 2:1-11 gives us some background, and reveals the part she played in God's great plan to deliver His people. Although she lived in a terrible time for the Israelites as a nation, she was reared in a truly God-loving and God-fearing family. Her family history was great. She was descended from the Levites, and they were spiritual people. She had so much going for her.

When her mother asked her to stand guard over her baby brother's basket, she obediently accepted the responsibility of guarding him, which was no small risk for a child to take. She had courage and lots of it. She was self-sacrificing to give of her playtime to see that no harm came to her brother. She measured up to her mother's expectations and all went well due to Miriam's quick thinking. When her baby brother cried and drew the princess' attention, Miriam went to get her mother and introduced her to the princess as a possible nurse.

The picture of Miriam in Exodus 15:20-21 also gives a glowing report of her. We see her as a talented, middle-aged woman who is being used by the Lord in various ways. It seems she chose to stay single to be free to minister, but even if it wasn't by her own choice, she accepted it. The prophet Micah indicates that she had a place of leadership with her two brothers, Moses and Aaron (Mic. 6:4). She was influential in inspiring the other women to sing as they marched toward the Promised Land and to praise God for all He had done for the Israelites. All is well to this point. The words of Psalm 69:30-31 could have been used to describe her: *"I will praise the Name of God with a song, and will magnify Him with thanksgiving. This also shall please the Lord better than an ox or bullock that hath horns and hoofs."*

The next time we see her name in print, however, is in the fearsome chapter of Numbers 12:1-16. Miriam is influencing people in a harmful way rather than inspiring them to praise the Lord, as she did previously. Her tongue is wagging in criticism against her brother Moses and his wife.

What went wrong? What caused her to change? Was it simply a critical attitude toward him, or was it a deeper problem? She was unhappy about Moses' marriage. Am I being too critical in thinking that she felt God wasn't being fair in His dealings with her and Aaron? Her little brother, the baby she had protected, was given a higher place of authority than she and Aaron had been given. I don't know for sure, but I'm inclined to think the problem involved more than the color of his wife's skin.

At any rate, once Miriam started to slip, the next step down came easily. Jealousy, envy, bitterness, dissatisfaction, and grumbling tumbled out in rapid succession. She seemed to have forgotten that God was listening to everything she said. If she had been more aware of the truth, she surely would not have expressed her complaints quite so freely. It never occurred to her that she might be wrong in her judgment. She felt discriminated against and believed Moses was getting away with something she didn't think he should. Perhaps many of us can sympathize with Miriam's feelings.

God did not like what He was hearing, however. He made it clear to her that He had chosen Moses as leader. Her actions displeased the Lord so much that He withdrew His glory from the whole nation. By afflicting her with the dreadful disease of leprosy, He let her know that He was deeply offended with her bad attitude. God called a halt to the march of perhaps two million souls to the Promised Land in order to discipline one woman who was definitely out of line.

God asked her where her fear of Him was. She had momentarily forgotten the truth expressed in Psalm 89:7: *"God is greatly to be feared in the assembly of the saints, and to be had in reverence of all them that are about Him."*

In a conversation about Miriam, I was once asked why God didn't chastise Aaron by making him a leper, too. After all, he had agreed with her criticism. Didn't that make him as guilty as she? No. Aaron, although he had been influenced by Miriam's criticism, admitted that Moses had been chosen by God for leadership. The next time he addressed Moses, he called him "lord" (not in capital letters) and accepted his position of leadership over him. By submitting to God's order, Aaron was spared being made a public example as Miriam had been.

Throughout Scripture, leprosy is a type of sin, so the reason the Lord chose that disease is apparent. The sins of the tongue spread as readily as the disease of leprosy. This is true in our time as well. What went through Miriam's mind as she sat alone outside the camp? It must have been quite a shock to go from being in the limelight to being an outcast. The remedy worked, and the Lord gave His permission to let her rejoin the camp as they started their journey again. God would not have allowed Miriam to rejoin the people of God if she had not had a repentant heart.

Through her repentance, God forgave her. However, it is sobering to me to realize that Miriam's name does not appear again in this story even though she had been accepted back into the circle of God's people. After her death, when Moses spoke to the people (Deut. 24:8-9) he used Miriam as an example, warning them not to forget the lesson learned through the experience.

I can never think I have it made. Miriam permitted the little things in life to spoil the fruit of the Spirit that she could

133

have borne for God. Does this thought challenge you as it did me? If Miriam, who had risen to such spiritual heights in godly maturity, can be tempted and slip so badly, surely I can, too. Solomon reminds us in Song of Solomon 2:15: *"Take us the foxes, the little foxes, that spoil the vines; for our vines have tender grapes."*

Let's not permit the damaging foxes to ruin the fruit of the Spirit before it matures.

28
HANG ON TO MY JACKET

I gasped at what was happening! My five-year-old was in trouble. We were in downtown Tokyo, picking up literature at a small Christian bookstore. I'd been driving around waiting for Gifford and our little daughter to come out of the store. I watched them from the opposite side of the street, saw them leave the shop and start to cross the busy, eight-lane road. Assuming by his gestures that Gifford—his own hands full of packages—had told her to hang on tightly to his jacket, I waited for them to cross. All went well for the first half of their crossing, but the signal light was too short to make it all the way, so they stopped at the island to wait. However, when the light changed and cars started up again, my daughter became very frightened. She panicked when she saw the cars whizzing by and heard all the noise. Letting go of Gifford's jacket, she made a dash across the street to our waiting car.

My heart still skips a beat as I recall the horror of those few seconds. I was petrified as I watched her run across a busy street against traffic. I was helpless to save her. Turning every which way, cars slammed to a halt with tires squealing. Nothing short of a miracle of God's protection can explain the avoidance of a serious traffic accident. Not only did she make it unscathed, not one car got even a scratch. Horror on the faces of drivers changed to smiles as they saw my little blonde girl run sobbing into my arms. By that time I was crying too, from sheer relief and happiness.

This incident brings to mind another heart-stopping episode in Tokyo. We were returning from an afternoon meeting and found ourselves swallowed up in a crowd of thousands of baseball fans rushing home after a game. The station platform swarmed with people who impatiently pushed forward to get into the train. Two guests were with us, which made us a party of seven, so we let several trains go by in an effort to stay together. The pushers, who were hired to pack a few more people onto each train, only added to the confusion. After strict instruction from Dad to get on the next train, we pushed forward through the nearest open doors.

We made it, but as the doors shut, I spied our eight-year old still standing in the crowd on the platform! She was the picture of dejection and fear. Horrified, I thought of our little girl separated from her parents and alone in that crowd of strangers. The six of us got off the train at the next station, desperately wondering what to do next. We prayed that the Lord would give us wisdom for how to make contact with her.

As we disembarked from the train, we heard our names being paged. The stationmaster met us with the instructions that we were to wait while one of the railway employees accompanied our daughter to this station. I had my doubts that she would go with him, because we had previously told our girls that should they ever be separated from us, they were to wait where they were and we would come to find them. We wondered if she would remember to follow our orders, so Gifford and our guests stayed where they were while I went back to see if she was waiting as she had been instructed to do.

When I arrived at the previous station, our daughter was screaming in hysteria, but she was still there! The station manager was trying to convince her to get on the train. In exasperation, he told me that he had never seen such a stubborn child! When I explained to him our previous agreement, however, he changed his assessment. It was a happy reunion when we once again boarded the next train and headed home together.

With three girls come three stories. On one of our trips Stateside, knowing it would be at least five years before we returned, our family drove into Chicago to make a few more purchases before leaving for Japan. The time passed quickly and we were not aware that it was closing time in the store. While we were paying for our purchases, the lights blinked in warning and we called the girls. It was our three-and-a-half-year-old who gave us a fright that time. All three girls had been there the minute before, but our mischievous, youngest daughter had picked that moment to play a game of hide-and-seek. In a split second she had disappeared!

When I heard no answer to my calling for her, I panicked. The first thing that flashed into my mind was that she had been kidnapped, so I ran out of the store to see if I could find her. When I turned around to reenter the store, the doors had already been locked! I could not get a single employee to answer my desperate calls until I spotted a clerk who was leaving the store. By this time, I was on the verge of hysteria. The clerk let us in and the remaining staff was sent to search for our daughter as they called her name on the intercom. Finally she was found under a desk, eating candy that a clerk had given her. She was happy and carefree as a lark, but I'm sure her innocent fun took another ten years off my life.

A similar thread can be seen in each of these stories. One of our girls had panicked, let go of her father's jacket, and had run from safety into the path of danger. She could not see that her father had a reason for waiting on the island for the light to change. Another daughter, paralyzed by her fear of the crowd, had lagged behind and momentarily lost our protection. This is another form of letting go of the jacket, isn't it? The third daughter merely wanted to let go and do her own thing. The result in all three cases could have been very serious had not God intervened.

At desperate times like these, when our loved ones are in physical danger, it is natural to instantly pray for their physical safety. Yet we also need prayer for situations that may appear to be far less desperate, but can be even more dangerous. I think, for example, of the times I've run from my Father's loving protection when I have panicked. I recall times

137

I've lagged behind and frozen in fear at certain of His commands. And I must admit, there have been times when I've been under the desk doing my own thing, too. We should be just as sensitive, urgently praying for help when we or our loved ones are in danger through spiritual immaturity.

We need to walk close enough to our heavenly Father that we walk when He walks, wait when He waits, and go forward when He goes forward. This requires perfect agreement in obedience with Him (Amos 3:3). As I read through the Scriptures, I see dozens of stories of people who took their hands off their heavenly Father's jacket (figuratively speaking) and found themselves in grave danger. Some did it only momentarily, and others did it for longer periods of time, but in each case the results were the same: spiritual disaster and the loss of God's direction and blessing.

Rebekah is one example of this (Gen. 27). Her mind was so full of the blessing she coveted for her beloved son that she could see no way ahead for him. She took things into her own hands, not waiting for God's time and method. As a result of her impetuous actions, she never saw Jacob again.

As I reflect back on the highway of life, I can see that the time waiting—whether for half a minute, half an hour or a lifetime—is not wasted time. There is a purpose in everything that God permits to happen to us. May we keep our hands on our Father's jacket as we walk down the road together, and may we encourage our loved ones to do the same. As parents we wanted our girls happy, but we were far more interested in their safety. This only came through their development, learning to accept such commands as "wait," "go," and "come." This creates security, happy living, and peace.

138

29
WHY DO YOU STUDY THE BIBLE?

Have you ever been asked why you study the Bible? When I was asked that question, I wondered what the instigator of the question had in mind. Did the questioner mean "study" or "read"? Although the answer to either question seemed obvious to me, there must have been a special reason for asking it, so I carefully thought before giving my answer. I replied by saying, "I read the Bible for my own enjoyment, nourishment, and to keep up my spiritual strength. Reading it daily is a necessity because I run out of steam very quickly and need to keep in touch with my Source of power. On the other hand, I study the Bible in preparation for teaching others and answering their questions. My Bible is my most valued and precious possession."

Perhaps the main reason for reading the Word is to get acquainted with the Author. It is of utmost importance to know the God represented in the Bible, not the one I have imagined in my own mind. I want to make sure the God I serve and worship is the God who made me, controls me, and has a right to dictate my behavior. I want to know without doubt that Jesus is the Person He claims to be—the anointed and prophesied One who alone can forgive sin through His precious blood. It is important that I have confidence in the gospel I share with others (as spoken by Paul in Galatians 1:6-9), and not another gospel of my own making. This knowledge is conveyed as we read the Bible.

Fifty-six years ago, letters began to arrive at our house, and with great eagerness I opened the first one. After I recognized the penmanship, I was even more eager to open the subsequent ones. At first they arrived a week apart, then three or four days apart. Then two arrived in the same mail. The remark our mailman made as he handed them to me is still fresh in my mind, "Why don't you marry the guy to save him postage?" I quickly assured him that I was doing all I could to hasten the day!

I could hardly open those letters fast enough. It required no effort whatsoever because I wanted to become even better acquainted with the author. No matter how many letters came, my eagerness did not wane. Before long, the mailman asked me again how things were progressing, and I assured him they were going first rate.

He teased me, "Be sure to invite me to the wedding!" He, his wife, and their three children all came. It was a joyous occasion, and I wanted to introduce them to the young man who had written all those letters and kept out mailman so busy. The author of the letters proved many times over to be a man I could trust and into whose hands I could confidently place my future. As Christians, we should look forward to reading the Bible as eagerly as I looked forward to reading letters from someone I loved.

Another reason for reading the Word is cleansing. We wouldn't think of beginning a day without washing our faces or brushing our teeth. Spiritually, we need to do the same thing. Isaiah 52:11 expresses this need well: *"Be ye clean, that bear the vessels of the Lord."*

The priests in Old Testament times had to stop at the laver for cleansing before they could serve or worship at the tabernacle or temple. The laver stood in the courtyard as a reminder for them to cleanse themselves from the dust that clung to their hands and feet. They needed cleansing physically from the pollution around them. In an even greater way, I feel the need for cleansing from the filth and pollution around me. As a New Testament priest, I must be no less clean spiritually than the Old Testament priests were required to be clean physically before serving or worshiping God.

I also read the Bible to discover my roots. I appreciate knowing all four of my grandparents arrived in America from Holland. However, to discover my roots many more generations back is far more important and that information is in the Bible. Through the Scriptures, I can trace my roots back to the creation of our world—back to Someone who was there from the beginning and has the story straight.

By reading the Bible, I also learn God's truth. Gifford and I shared many a good laugh after a missionary presentation while we were in the United States on furlough. After giving a message, he was often asked questions about Japan, the people, and the work. I sat in the audience and once in a while I had differing ideas about how to answer the same questions. We both lived in Japan, but we had different impressions of the same situations.

The Lord, however, has His facts right. Truth is whatever God says about anything. It never has to be revised because it never changes. God never reads a situation wrongly as we often do.

God gave us His Word in a way that is both clear and complicated. Because it is clear, it encourages even the newest believer; because it is complicated, it keeps us seeking to find the fullness of His truth. It really is exciting to me how the Bible dove-tails together so beautifully. I see God's plan for man unfold as He works and dwells among His people through the millenniums. Finding new truths from time to time renews my interest in God and His work. Reading one portion of Scripture helps explain another. It is my prayer, as I read the Bible year after year, that I will constantly increase my understanding and appreciation of God and His Son Jesus Christ. I want to become a true worshiper in spirit and in truth.

Now, to answer the original question of why I study the

Bible, I have to admit that my main incentive is to help other people understand it in order to acquaint them with God and His Son. Teaching the Word requires a great deal of study in order to be able to rightly divide the Word of Truth and accurately answer questions regarding it.

My own faith always gets a fresh boost when I think back to a conversation at our dinner table one night when my father was talking about the Jewish people. This conversation took place well over sixty years ago and nearly ten years before Israel became a nation. My father said that Israel would go back to the Promised Land and become established as a nation. He also revealed many other facts of prophecy—all of which have been fulfilled exactly as the Bible said they would be. My dad didn't have a special gift of prophecy, but he did have a knowledge of the Word because he had studied it diligently. It was especially thrilling when I visited Israel to see many of the places Dad had talked about so often. My only regret is not paying better attention and learning more from him about these precious truths. We all need to take Paul's admonition in 1 Timothy 4:13 more seriously: *"Till I come, give attendance to reading, to exhortation, to doctrine."*

Reading the Scriptures is as necessary as giving milk to a baby. Paul states in Romans 10:17: *"Faith cometh by hearing, and hearing by the Word of God."*

I've been told that seniors also need milk—which doesn't surprise me a bit because I constantly need my faith to be strengthened. One would think after sixty-six years of walking by faith it wouldn't need to be tested so often. But I don't know how many more "proofs" I am going to need after seeing God provide and protect in so many unbelievable ways.

Studying the Bible on the other hand, is more than milk. It is branching out into the "solid food" of spiritual life. The author of Hebrews explains the reason for the solid food—to learn discernment: *"But solid food belongeth to them that are of full age, even those who by reason of use have their senses exercised to discern both good and evil"* (Heb. 5:14).

Our spiritual walk is not a leisurely stroll. We need the nourishment of Scripture and the support of others to complete the journey. This need brings to mind an embarrassing experience I once had in Japan. I started out with a group of much younger people for a picnic lunch atop a "small" mountain. Since they assumed I could make it to the top, I did too. But when we arrived at the trailhead, it looked more like Mt. Fuji than a small mountain, and I had great doubts. I was in a difficult spot because I would spoil their whole day if I refused to go with them. They readily assured me that they would help me, so we started out, but it wasn't long before I was completely winded. I pleaded with my companions to go on ahead, promising to continue on at my own pace, and join them by lunchtime. (They had brought songbooks and Bibles, so I knew they planned a time of study before lunch.)

Well, the meeting ended and I still hadn't shown up! Becoming concerned about me, they started back down the trail to see if I was alright. One young fellow picked up a branch and told me to hang on to the end of it while he walked backwards in front of me, pulling me along. I had lived in Japan long enough to know that their culture wouldn't allow them to eat before I joined them, so I made a valiant effort to keep going and very shakily made it to the top. It really was worth the effort when I finally got to the top. We had our lunch together and enjoyed about an hour's rest before starting back down.

If you happen to be winded from the long, hard journey to the top of your spiritual life, I encourage you not to be too embarrassed or proud to grab a stick and let others help you. We are on this trek together. Above all, don't forget the nourishment for strength along the way. Paul's vocabulary regarding the spiritual life (struggle, endure, wrestle, fight) suggests that it is not a leisurely walk. It requires commitment, good nourishment, and the support of others, but the view from the top is breathtaking and well worth the struggle. Don't miss out on God's marvelous panoramic view of His purpose and plan for the ages. It is stretched out in His Word and it is ours to enjoy when we faithfully plod on in the reading and studying of it.

30
OUT OF THE MOUTHS OF BABES

One Saturday afternoon, a group of missionary children gathered in our living room. They were having a great time comparing notes on their parents, and I was in the kitchen preparing snacks for the group. Gifford had made my life easier by moving the original cold kitchen from the back of the house to a corner of the living room. He partitioned off a space for cupboards, leaving an open space at the top to allow heat from the kerosene stove in the living room to warm the kitchen space. So, I often overheard interesting conversations from my vantage point because I could not be seen, but I could hear all of the conversation clearly. Out of sight, out of mind, was the rule of the day.

As I heard one set of parents being compared to another, my interest increased. I stopped working to listen more intently. I soon recognized the voice of my young daughter starting to tell the group about her parents, and I didn't want to miss a word of it! The shock of my life came when I heard her share one simple sentence with the others: "You should hear the way my mom talks to my dad. It's awful." That's the only part of the conversation I can quote word for word. When one of the other children asked her what her father answered back, she told him that he never said anything. He just became quiet. Hurt and angry, I was ready to go out and let her have it with both barrels! I felt her statement was an extremely unjust lie. I did not have a sharp tongue!

If I had done this, however, I would have given them a living example of exactly what she was talking about. Instead, in the privacy of the kitchen, I began to ask the Lord if what she had said was true. Did I have a sharp tongue, or was it an exaggeration from a child's viewpoint? For the next few weeks, I took notice of everything I said to see if her accusation was really true. Several times I caught my tongue poised for an angry outburst.

Then I asked my husband if he felt that he had been made the target of my tongue. Fully expecting him to deny the fact, I was hardly prepared for his answer. He had been hurt many times and had been praying that the Lord would make me aware of how quickly I retorted. He explained that the tone of my voice sometimes hurt even more than the words themselves. After praying together, we both felt much better. I earnestly prayed that the words of my mouth would be acceptable in the Lord's sight as expressed in Psalm 19:14: *"Let the words of my mouth, and the meditation of my heart, be acceptable in Thy sight, O Lord, my Strength and my Redeemer."*

The Lord had used a child to bring my unruly tongue to my attention and cause me to feel the need to bring it under better control. The knowledge was painful at the time, and bringing it under control has been the battle of a lifetime.

Actually, my daughter's comment was not the first time I had been rebuked for not guarding what I said about others. During my late teens, a girlfriend with whom I worked in an office in Germantown, Pennsylvania, invited me home for dinner and to meet her husband. We had a lovely time at the table, then her husband retired to the living room to leave the two of us to talk. And talk we did! We had a lot to say about our boss until her husband called out from the other room saying that we should read our Bibles and put into practice 1 Thessalonians 4:11! We looked at each other in surprise, then we took his advice and read the verse: *"Study to be quiet, and to do your [our] own business, and to work with your [our] own hands, as we command you to do."*

At the time, I didn't take much stock in what he said. But in looking back, I can see that it was a reprimand from the Lord. I didn't particularly benefit from it and merely shrugged it off. Our conversation changed, and I soon left for home. I never really liked the man after that evening.

Another memory of being chastised goes back even farther, to my pre-teen days. A number of my young friends and I decided to visit an elderly widow who was a shut-in to "encourage her." Our mothers agreed that it was a very good idea and packed lunches for us since it was a walk of four miles one way and we would need the whole day to get there and back. We arrived right on schedule and ate lunch with the widow. It was a beautiful summer day. We had thoroughly enjoyed the countryside and were having a great time with this dear saint of God when she suddenly got up and hobbled to her bedroom.

She came back to us and opened her Bible to 1 John chapter 4 which she read to us emphasizing the word love each time it appeared. She ended with the admonition to put this portion into practice in our lives. She had noticed that our conversation at the table did not match our spirit of love in coming to visit her. We had discussed our friends who had not joined us, our school teachers, our Sunday school teachers, and our parents—raking them over the coals in childish chatter. We didn't particularly appreciate what she was trying to tell us. She said we needed to love others in the same way that God expresses His love for us and ended with the admonition to think about it and talk about it on the way home. I remember feeling hurt that day, too. I thought our mission of mercy had been a disaster, but her message made enough of an impression on me that I remember it clearly to this day.

Martha has often been an inspiration to me as I see how she accepted the Lord's correction (Lk 10:38-42). I would have been hurt and ashamed had I been corrected as she was in front of a houseful of guests. Yet Martha took Christ's chastisement and grew through it, changing from a troubled homemaker into a woman whom the Lord loved in a special way. In the very next chapter of Luke, we see her serving tables again. I had only been rebuked in front of a dozen or so missionary children, and they hadn't been able to see my reaction. (I never mentioned it to any of them.)

Now, I often imagine Martha drawing alongside of me and reminding me to read Hebrews 12. There is a strong correlation between the Lord's faithfulness in training us and our spiritual development. It is evident that Martha took the rebuke from the Lord as chastisement and benefitted from it in the manner of Hebrews 12:11: *"Now no chastening for the present seemeth to be joyous, but grievous; nevertheless, afterward it yieldeth the peaceable fruit of righteousness unto them which are exercised thereby."*

Martha seems to have learned why the Lord chastised her, and I need to do the same. She listened to what Christ said, accepted it, and learned valuable truths. Because she did this, her faith was strengthened. She believed and, as a result, saw the glory of God when she witnessed the resurrection of her younger brother. Through her experience, we now have more details on the resurrection of the dead to encourage our hope in Christ.

Martha didn't retreat into a shell, nursing her injuries because the Lord embarrassed her before others. Because of her humble courage, her example is now powerful enough to: *"Lift up [my] hands which hang down, and the feeble knees; and make straight paths for [my] feet, lest that which is lame be turned out of the way"* (Heb. 12:12-13).

I am looking forward to finding Martha "one of these days" and telling her how thankful I am that she didn't deny needing what the Lord said to her. Instead of letting a root of bitterness grow in an unforgiving heart (v. 15), she took His advice and continued doing what she could to further His cause. She took to heart Psalm 141:5: *"Let the righteous smite me: it shall be a kindness: and let him reprove me: it shall be an excellent oil, which shall not break my head."*

We may not always like those whom God uses to rebuke us, but we would be wise to overlook the person whom God is using and take the chastisement as from Him. Then we will have much to think about on our way Home.

31
Counting the Cost

The trip back to Japan in the spring of 1999 was especially memorable because it was exactly fifty years since we arrived there the first time.

Before I went, I had asked that the schedule be an easy one which would allow a lot of time for fellowship with people individually. I wanted time to reminisce and gather a few more details of past events. I specifically asked that there be no large gatherings or celebrations. The end result of that plan was that I ended my visit with a feeling of awe at what God has done and how He has blessed families down to the third and fourth generations. I could only cry out, "Oh, God, Your keeping power is awesome! You truly have given grace sufficiently in keeping Christ's promise of Mark 8:34-35."

Those who chose to come to Him—losing their own lives to follow Him, truly have saved their lives while still here in this world. They have been able to lead others instead of stumbling them (as I so often worried they might). I blush to think of the times I worried for some of them, thinking God was asking too much. I often took the part of single sisters in their loneliness and special problems, thinking the way was too hard for them. I wondered how families could live when they gave up so much to put God and His work ahead of their own needs. I was rebuked over and over, and felt more than once that I wanted to put ashes on my head as Job did.

Occasion after occasion came to mind of decisions some of the Japanese believers were forced to make which I'd never faced in my lifetime, trials they had which were foreign to me.

I thought of one dear elderly sister who was saved while in the hospital. The first time we visited her after her release she was living comfortably in the home of her son and his family. But the next time we went, she was living out in a small building on the property by herself. When I asked why the change, she informed me that she had bowed her head to give silent thanks for her food to her new-found God. This action angered her son and he told her never to do so again. It was he who had worked for the food she ate, and he would appreciate her thanking him and leaving it at that.

She would not deny her Lord and Saviour in that manner. Thank God the son did not put her out on the street completely as he had threatened, but she did live on a meager income after that. The daughter-in-law would slip her special treats now and then, and had a fairly good relationship with her when the husband was not at home.

I thought of the young man whose father threw a cup of hot tea at him when he tried to witness to him about the necessity of having his sins forgiven. He was a good man and he had been a good father, it was true, but it didn't cancel out the sins of his heart and the son didn't want him deluded. He loved him too much for that, but the father was not able to see his son's witnessing as an evidence of love.

Another student's father grabbed his Bible away from him and threw it in the fire. The boy had to find odd jobs here and there to buy another one.

I know of three women who weathered bad marriages to unsaved men, even though they had been counseled to divorce their husbands. Because they wanted to keep their vows, they won their spouses to the Lord through consistent lives. They now have strong, happy marriages.

I recalled the agony of a kindergarten teacher as she had to tell her unsaved parents that she had been let go because she refused to take her pupils to the public shrine to teach them the proper protocol of worship and burning of incense. And of

152

a father of young children who gave up a responsible position because it necessitated working on the Lord's day.

Also, I remembered the trauma of a young couple signing over the rights he had as the oldest son to the homestead, giving it all over to his sister. They refused to assume the ancestral rites of the family rather than betray the Lord. The cost was much higher in some cases, but very real to them all.

None of these incidents was the result of natural disasters to be endured, but were the consequences of a definite choice to take up a cross in order to follow Christ. There is great advantage in accepting what God has permitted to happen, but it is more rewarding to purposefully count the cost of discipleship and then to suffer or bear loss for His name's sake.

From all outward evidence, not one of these Christians is any the worse off today as a result of not running away from suffering. In fact, the Lord's blessing was obvious through the happiness expressed and their eagerness to serve the Lord that God has honored them all. I came home with a greater desire to be more faithful myself in serving the Lord.

32
HIGHER AUTHORITY

I'm so glad it is the Lord that builds His house. He uses raw materials that at first seem sub-standard at best. Yet in no way is He hindered in the final results by human weaknesses. He uses man's limitations and His strengths to produce it in His time, using a variety of people to get just the right balance. I'm thinking right now of plural leadership in the local church.

I was impressed especially during my last visit to Japan how this is true and I can see now why there were times we had to "put up" with situations much to our disliking, but we needed them all to keep us in balance. There were times when young people complained that some elders were too strict; others, we thought often overlooked more than they should have. Some stressed works too much; others almost completely ignored them in the life of believers, placing all the responsibility for our behavior on Christ.

The seed for my thoughts came through the story of the centurion whose servant was healed, found in Matthew 8:5-13. The following story came to mind as I could see that God uses men with different family backgrounds to mold them for leadership. My association with a dear brother goes back about forty years, beginning when he was a high school student. As we met the family and got to know them, we could see why his background has had such a strong influence on his Christian life. I often marveled at the immediate obedience he gave to his parents. His father was a retired military general, and when he returned from the war he carried over the authority and demeanor of a general, expecting the boy to obey as his men had. Yet we sensed an unusual love on the part of the father for his son. We thought of him as another Jacob with a son in his old age. The boy was born after the war when the older children were leaving home.

The parents loved their youngest, and at the same time had great expectations and dreams for him to do well in life. They pushed him academically and demanded more than the average from him. Either the father or the mother would constantly call us when they suspected he was at our house having a good time ("wasting his time") with all the other young people. He used to look at me as I answered the phone, smile, take the phone and say the English equivalent of "Yes, Sir," jump on his bike and peddle home without question or argument.

Everything about this boy reflected politeness and respect. He had a strong character, but a very gentle manner. He could hold his own and still be nice about it. I might add that this characteristic carried over into his spiritual convictions as well. We saw this after his conversion when the issue of the rituals at the family shrine were concerned. The day came when he had to say "No" to the father and explain carefully and lovingly to him that he now had to follow a higher authority when it came to spiritual issues. In all the other phases of life he responded in submission to his father.

He was grateful that his parents were paying his school bills, but he was prepared to drop out of school if it required compromise with idols. He even went so far as to make it clear to his parents that he would someday have to answer to the Person in Higher Authority and would have to bow his knees to Him as well—and so would they. He explained that he respected both of them, but that he feared God more because He had an authority which superceded that invested by the Japanese government. Needless to say, this was not received too happily, but they respected his convictions and they knew only too well that human goverments fail at times.

He did not have to drop out of school. As long as the par-

ents were well, the issue was not urgent. He used every opportunity he felt was appropriate to give them the gospel. Instead
of stumbling the parents, their respect for him grew.

Years later, one surprising day came when the father heard
of Gifford's terminal illness and agreed to a visit with him. If I
remember correctly, it was Gifford's last visit to anyone's
home. An elderly man now, it was very evident that the gentleman's heart was well prepared by the Holy Spirit. We had a
great visit. As we were getting ready to leave, the father said
to Gifford that at New Year's that year he had had the feeling
that it was going to be a special year for him. Since then he had
thought much about the matter of God's authority, and His
power to carry out discipline. He recognized, as the centurion
in Scripture did, that Christ has all the powers behind Him of
the Godhead while He was still in human flesh. The day came
when he received and accepted that Authority as his Saviour.

I can still see that farewell vividly—watching the two men
try to stand to their feet, the one weakened by age, the other
by severe sickness. It took two of us to get Gifford on his feet,
but his heart was as light as a feather.

Over the years, we have thanked the Lord many times for
the steady character of this dear brother. He saw the truth and
contended for it. He was faithful through thick and thin. He
accepted the Bible and the God of the Bible as his sole authority from the very day he was saved. He stood up for the truth
even when he was all alone. We could always count on his
support for anything backed by the Scriptures. What a choice
gift he has been to the churches! His contribution has not only
been from the platform, but in his personal counselling. His
influence covers a wide area and others respect his advice.

The father made a confession of faith soon after this incident, but it took several years before the mother trusted the
Lord. I was struck in realizing that the strict military training
of his father built character and stability. God has used this
firm and faithful trait to bring the parents to the Lord.

157

33
A GOOD SOLDIER OF JESUS CHRIST

I'm so glad that God is not the stuffy, hard to please Person I imagined Him to be the first few years after salvation. I'm also thankful that He's not the wish-washy God I was hoping He was, so I could manipulate Him into doing what I wanted Him to do. And I'm certainly grateful that He didn't always run things the way I felt best in the work of the Lord. For His ways are past finding out; they always prove to work out the best and for the benefit of everyone involved—though sometimes it takes many years to discover this truth.

I'm thinking right now of an evangelist who more or less commended himself to the work of the Lord, not because he felt he was worthy, but rather that he had such a burden he had to get on with the job. He was commended in the scriptural way afterwards—through the elders, but God proved Himself very real in response to his heartfelt desire to serve Him soon after conversion. It may not have been the way to do it, but God certainly has put His hand of blessing on him and the work he has accomplished with the Lord's help.

This young man was an outstanding person with the promise of being successful in whatever field he chose. He had already worked himself up in one company, and had left home to rent an apartment for himself in a neighboring city. Meeting a missionary living there, he became a believer in the Lord Jesus. He grew by leaps and bounds in the knowledge of the Bible and in his desire to lead people to Christ. It wasn't long after he was saved before he decided to become an evangelist and go into the Lord's work full-time. He asked for a month's leave of absence from his work, and told the Lord he would work for Him as long as He took care of him in meeting his needs (sounds like Jacob, see Gen. 28:20). Things were going as planned until the last day of his agreement with God. He had completely run out of supplies, night time was drawing close and he still had had no dinner that evening. He would tell no one of his need, so he prayed that the Lord would send something in yet during the evening.

He was really puzzled at this turn of events and how this testing time was ending. When 8:30 came and still nothing nor any provision to buy anything with, he decided that he would go back to work. Before nine o'clock there was a knock on his door. His neighbor had a large plate in her hand of "osashimi," or raw fish on rice paddies. She explained that they had invited guests and they never showed up. She couldn't bear to think of the food going to waste and asked him if he wanted it. The Lord had not only provided him with a meal, but it was one of Japan's best.

With that fresh encouragement, he quit his secular employment and put his whole heart into witnessing to others. He began in his own family. His older sister was experiencing one of the most difficult trials any woman can bare, that of losing a toddler. The little fellow had fallen into the bath and drowned. It was a case of adding grief upon grief for she not only had lost her oldest son, but the police interrogated her to the breaking point, accusing her of carelessness. They suspected her of being guilty of child neglect and accused her as if it was all her fault. Even harder to take was the misunderstanding of family and friends, especially her mother-in-law. Her brother, however, spent a great deal of time in comforting her and giving her the gospel.

As they read the Bible together, he explained that God had been there when the death of her child happened, and that God was sovereign. He could have prevented the accident, but He didn't. Therefore He had a greater purpose. He not only

160

could save her and prepare her to go to heaven herself, but that her child would be there as well (2 Sam. 12:23).

Through this message he explained the power of sin and how Satan, as an enemy of God, was trying to destroy her eternal soul in getting her to follow him instead of yielding her life to God. He read to her the horrors of hell and that God was drawing her to Himself. He wanted her to share eternity with Him rather than having to suffer forever in hell. He told her that no suffering she endured in this life was worthy to be compared with the joys of heaven. She responded to the Holy Spirit's guiding, and believed what he told her. She accepted Christ as her personal Saviour. Together they began speaking to their mother who was also suffering with her.

The mother also accepted the message of God's supreme control in the affairs of their lives, and was born again. The son then began commuting weekly to his hometown and started weekly cottage meetings to reach the rest of his family. A few neighbors also attended this meeting, but the father would arrange to be gone each week. On one occasion when the father returned home, he heard sobbing coming from an upstairs room. Quietly climbing the stairs, he found the young man prostrate on the floor pouring out his heart to the Lord for the salvation of his father. He gently touched the young man's shoulder and asked him what was wrong.

The son blurted out that if the father did not accept the salvation God provided through his Son, Jesus Christ, he would not be able to enter heaven with him, with his sister and mother. The father began to ask why he felt so strongly about his beliefs concerning God, and what assurance he had that what he believed was true. Above all, why would he, the father, be excluded?

The fact of sin was very repulsive to him and he resisted the teaching of the necessity of the shedding of Christ's blood. He was a good man and did not believe he was a sinner. It just didn't fit into his thinking. Never backing down, the son pleaded with his father to look further into the matter. He agreed to do this and also came to a saving knowledge of Christ. It wasn't too long afterward that his younger sister and other brothers also became Christians. By this time a small fellowship of believers was formed as the young man and the missionary worked together in the spreading of the gospel.

The son was still not satisfied and began to bring up not keeping the family shrine which represented the family religion. This subject also made the father extremely uncomfortable. To add Christianity was one thing, but to replace entirely what he had always believed and practiced was quite another story. This, too, was a battle within his soul for months, but finally one day his wife decided to help him in this decision, so she took the family shrine outside. It had already been taken from its honored place, but she split it up and put it piece by piece in the firebox of the tub. When he finished his lovely, warm bath she asked him how he enjoyed it. His response was that he had never enjoyed one better.

She then held her breath as she told him it had been fired with wood from the shrine. Instead of anger she was prepared to receive, the dear gentleman relaxed as if he was glad the battle was over and never regretted her actions once since then either. In fact he later joked over the fact that he felt cleaner than ever after that bath. It seems to me that the joy experienced in salvation is largely in proportion to the cost paid in receiving it. This is certainly not the end of his story, but it is of mine for this time.

34
GOD'S GREAT POWER

There are few things which send a warm feeling through me more than catching the eye of an old friend and seeing her face light up. It was our second Lord's Day on our recent visit to Japan and we were visiting a neighboring assembly when a very special lady walked in. She was a friend of many years. The service had not started yet. It is amazing how Christians can start a conversation where they left off as if time had not existed. The circumstances and incidences that brought us together the first time we met were not the ordinary ones.

I had received a phone call in the afternoon from a sister in the church telling me that an insurance agent she knew was extremely interested in the gospel. The Christian had been witnessing to her for weeks and she felt the need of reinforcements. She had made a date to visit the lady in her home that evening and asked me to accompany her. I agreed to go.

I had no idea what we would find when we got there. To my amazement, the woman's high school daughter rushed out of the house to meet us. Not even waiting for an introduction, she excitedly told us that her English teacher had told them a story *that very day* a about a missionary living in Takasaki, a Mr. Beckon. Then when she got home, she heard from her mother that Mrs. Beckon was to come that evening. She was so anxious to meet me and couldn't get over the coincidence.

We went inside, sat at the low table in the middle of the room, and had tea and snacks. After the usual chit-chat, we settled down to serious talk. Not too long after, the insurance agent's husband joined the four of us, showing interest, too.

I opened my Bible to the second chapter of John and read about the marriage in Cana at which Christ had changed water into wine. I made several comments, but when I made the statement that the Lord could change the water of everyday life into wine which is a symbol of joy, the husband hurriedly rose and left the room. I wondered if he had been offended. Within minutes he was back holding a Bible. He said that he had something to show us that we might not believe if he only told us. He wanted me to see it with my own eyes. My late husband had said those exact words many years before at a Bible class the husband attended in high school and he had made a note of it by the verse. Sure enough, I had even used Gifford's exact words! The fact that he had attended a Bible class was news to everyone present, and a surprise that he should remember the comment.

The husband had recently suffered a heart attack which had caused him to think much about death and eternity. He had remembered more from the Bible Class and had been reading a bit from the Bible on his own. His heart definitely was prepared by God for the conversation that night. He had also heard a lot from his wife who related to him what my friend had been telling her about God, His Son Jesus Christ, and the problem of sin. As a result of the happenings of that evening the family began attending the services at the assembly and in the process of time were saved and baptized.

This year, seeing the earnestness with which this dear lady—now a widow—worshipped the Lord spoke volumes to me. It made me thankful to have the opportunity to visit Japan again. To experience the power of God to this extent, seeing the way He used so many people, especially a woman buying up her opportunity to witness, the timing and even the passages read to bring it all about, forcefully verified Philippians 2:13, *"For it is God which worketh in you both to will and to do of His good pleasure."*

35
A Tour Guide Flag

Seeing three generations of believers under one roof caused my soul to cry out, "Oh God, my God, how great thou art!" The cults can boast of great buildings, miracles, and large growth in numbers, but only the true God can work in people's lives as I observed, keeping them happily together, weeding out character flaws, and inspite of human weaknesses making us strong. Around the dinner table my memory file opened wide and the story of the struggles of individuals who were present began to pour out.

We were looking at the video of the funeral of the elder brother's wife, the mother and grandmother of those present. His entire family was present, but I could enjoy my own thoughts as the atmosphere was quiet and respectful. Only the background noise of happy children could be heard.

I wasn't required to make conversation, so I could review the women's prayer meetings where the wife had prayed earnestly for the salvation of her husband and for the spiritual growth of those of her children who were already saved. I thought back to the times the sons battled with choices of education and later the strong opposition they felt while away in university. I recalled several visits with Gifford when he looked them up, seeking to help them with their doubts, generated by ungodly professors. Then, of their selections of partners in marriage.

Their children left home about the same time that ours did to seek lives on their own. We parents had to cope with the same adjustments and they found it as hard to let each go as we did ours, but John 10:4 proved true in every case: *"And when He putteth forth His own sheep, He goes before them, and the sheep follow Him; for they know His voice."*

The Shepherd went before them all as they went out to pasture. I can even remember the tinge of jealousy I felt that their children seemed to have fewer battles with common doubts of faith and were strong in resisting compromise with the world. The following, and the hearing of His voice, was true with each individual.

That evening, as we parents could see the power of a Great God in keeping watch over His own sheep, I could envision the second generation passing under His rod for counting, caressing and care, and I was reminded of my responsibility to pray for the third and the coming fourth generation. The elderly gentleman now carries the burden of prayer alone for his family, and it is a heavy one. Please give him a hand and include many other Christian grandparents in Japan.

Seeing the video was a thrill to me. Because of their wide influence on their whole community, he, his oldest son, and an evangelist had the privilege of preaching to hundreds of unsaved about the necessity to prepare to meet their God. In a land where the teaching of reincarnation is prevalent, the message of Hebrews 9:27 is important, *"It is appointed unto men once to die, but after this the judgment."*

One unique feature on the video which caught my eye immediately was the wife's favorite chair on the stage surrounded by flowers and her Bible open resting on it. It was a silent but eloquent challenge to every believing mother to faithfully pray for her family. The happy time of fellowship that night proved again to me the power of those prayers, and it encouraged me to continue praying. It also reminded me that our role as grandparents is great. The song, "Happy the Home Where Jesus Lives" came to mind. In this home He has been dear to every heart, and it showed.

It is strange what images pass before one's mind, but at the

World's Fair in Osaka many years ago, I saw many a tour guide walking about with a flag lifted in the air, leading groups of people to various exhibits and then safely back to their buses. I viewed this dear Christian as a tour guide walking through life with a flag in his hand, pointing the way.

He is a true gentleman in every sense of the word, with a helpful, pleasing personality. His gentle spirit has helped so many people through life's crises. He is definitely not a crusader and sometimes we even wished he would express himself more forcefully, but many people have been attracted to attend gospel services because of his testimony. His wife's funeral was just another one of those times and the flag he holds has the name of Jesus Christ in bold print. He uses it to lead people the way to eternity.